THE BIG BOOK OF SOCCER

BY **MUNDIAL**

ILLUSTRATED BY
DAMIEN WEIGHILL

WIDE EYED EDITIONS

CONTENTS

INTRODUCTION   4

THE BASICS AND THE LINGO   6

HISTORY OF SOCCER   10

THE GAME THROUGH TIME   12

THE GREATEST TEAMS OF ALL TIME   14

SOCCER CLEATS PAST TO PRESENT   20

THE EVOLUTION OF THE BALL   22

THE GREAT PLAYERS   24

LEGENDARY COACHES AND HOW THEY DID IT 32

THE KEY POSITIONS   34

COACHES AND FORMATIONS   36

THE BIG CUPS   42

AMAZING STADIUMS 50

COOLEST UNIFORMS   58

HOW TO...   66

TAKE THE PERFECT SHOT LIKE JI SO-YUN   68

MAKE THE PERFECT SLIDE TACKLE LIKE ALESSANDRO NESTA   70

TAKE THE PERFECT SET PIECE LIKE DAVID BECKHAM   72

PLAY THE PERFECT LONG BALL LIKE XABI ALONSO   74

TAKE PENALTIES LIKE MATT LE TISSIER 76

DO NUTMEGS LIKE LUIS SUÁREZ   78

HAVE THE PERFECT FIRST TOUCH LIKE DENNIS BERGKAMP 80

PLAY THE PERFECT THROUGH BALL LIKE XAVI 82

BEAT THE OFFSIDE TRAP LIKE FERNANDO TORRES   83

DO THE PERFECT ATTACKING HEADER LIKE DIDIER DROGBA   84

DO THE PERFECT DEFENSIVE HEADER LIKE KALIDOU KOULIBALY   86

WEIRD AND WONDERFUL   88

THE HAIRCUTS   90

THE CELEBRATIONS   92

THE BIGGEST, THE BEST, AND THE WEIRDEST   96

A STIR-FRIED AIRPLANE   98

MORE THAN THE GAME   100

RESPECTING THE REF   102

THE OTHER JOBS   104

THE GAME DAY   106

THE CROWD   108

INDEX   110

DO YOU LOVE SOCCER? OF COURSE YOU DO! This book is here to help you fall in love with it even more and arm you with some crucial knowledge as well as practical tips to improve your own game.

In this book, you will find unbelievable stories, strange haircuts, genius tactics, and huge stadiums. You will meet the best teams, players, and coaches of all time. You will learn the lingo and get the lowdown on how to perfect skills and moves just like the pros who made them famous.

You are about to find out more about the greatest sport ever invented than any of your friends have ever known. You are about to see what it takes to become the best soccer player in the world.

This book will show you how to enjoy every second of soccer, even when you don't think you're enjoying it. Even when your team loses in the last minute and you feel like giving up. It will help you remember the good, the bad, and the funny times. We soccer fans are fantastic and ridiculous, but most importantly, we're all in it together.

LET'S GO.

THE BASICS AND THE LINGO

Soccer is the best sport in the world because it's the simplest. From Brazil to Belgium, Bangladesh to Botswana, soccer is being played in every corner of the planet. Whether it's on a field, in the street outside your house, or in the park down the road, you can play it anywhere.

All you need is a ball, or something that looks sort of like a ball. You can score great goals, make amazing passes, and even win the World Cup (in your head) with a tennis ball, a bunch of scrunched-up adhesive tape, or a pair of socks. Anybody, anywhere, anytime can play it.

BASIC LINGO

Here are the key phrases that will get you talking like a soccer expert in no time.

ASSIST A pass, header, or cross that comes just before a goal is scored. The German player Mesut Özil is the king of this.

BACKHEEL A pass played with the back of a player's foot.

BICYCLE KICK With the ball behind them, a player throws their body into the air, makes a movement with the legs to get one in front of the other, and connects with the ball to hit it over their head while in midair. Also known as an overhead kick.

BRACE Two goals scored by the same player in one game.

CAPTAIN The captain of the team is the leader on the field. They are chosen by the coach or manager. You can recognize the captain by the armband they wear.

CHIP Chipping the goalkeeper is when an attacker kicks the ball over the top of a goalkeeper's head and into the goal. When it works, it makes the person shooting look fantastic.

CLEAN SHEET If a goalkeeper does not concede a goal (let a goal into the net), they have kept a "clean sheet." Before computers, scores would be recorded on a sheet of paper. And so, if the opposition didn't score, the sheet would be clean.

CORNER KICK

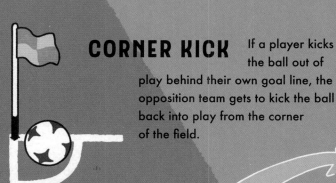

If a player kicks the ball out of play behind their own goal line, the opposition team gets to kick the ball back into play from the corner of the field.

FOUL

When a player breaks the rules of the game. Punishable by a free kick or penalty.

CROSS

A delivery of the ball into the penalty area by the attacking team. Usually in the air, sometimes along the ground. England player David Beckham was the best at these.

FRIENDLY

A non-competitive game played between two teams just for fun or practice.

DRIBBLE

To run quickly with the ball at your feet.

HAT TRICK

If one player scores three goals in the same game.

EXTRA TIME

If the scores in a soccer game are even at full time, it is called a **draw**. Sometimes, if a game ends in a draw, the teams will play for an extra 30 minutes (on top of the 90 they've already played) to try and determine a winner.

KICKOFF

The very first kick of the game after the starting whistle blows.

FORMATION

This is the name given to the shape that a team takes during the game. For example, if a team plays four defenders, three central midfielders, two attacking midfielders, and one striker, it looks sort of like a Christmas tree, so it is called "the Christmas Tree Formation." 4-4-2 is the standard formation.

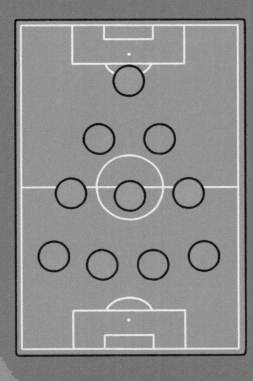

NUTMEG

When another player rolls the ball through your legs. Humiliating, but brilliant.

OFFSIDE

Being caught "offside" will result in the opposition being awarded a free kick. But what is it?

When your teammate passes the ball forward to you, there must be at least two opposition players between you and your opponent's goal at the moment your teammate passes. This is usually a defender and the goalkeeper. If there is only the goalkeeper between you and the goal at the moment the ball is passed to you, you are offside. If there is a defender and the goalkeeper between you and the goal when the ball is passed to you, you are onside.

ONSIDE | OFFSIDE

OWN GOAL

If you put the ball into the goal your team is defending, you have scored an "own goal." This counts as a goal for the opposition. Don't worry, we've all done it.

POSSESSION

When a team is in control of the ball.

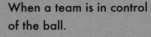

RED/ YELLOW CARD

A yellow card is a warning if you have committed a foul. If the referee shows you a red card, you have to leave the field, and you won't be allowed to play for the rest of the game. Two yellow cards have the same effect as a red card.

SHOOT

To "shoot" means to kick the ball at the opposition goal. You take a "shot" at the goal.

SAVE

A "save" is when a goalkeeper prevents the opposition from scoring by stopping a shot from going into their team's goal. They have "saved" their team. Thanks, goalie.

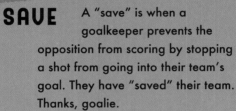

TACKLE

When you try to get the ball from another player.

STOPPAGE/ INJURY TIME

A normal soccer game lasts for 90 minutes. "Stoppage" or "injury" time is added to the end of a game to make up for the time when the game may have been stopped for any reason.

REFEREE

The person who is in charge of a game. They decide what counts as a foul or a goal, and they award red and yellow cards. If they blow their whistle, you have to stop playing and listen to what they say.

VOLLEY

When the ball is kicked before it has had a chance to bounce. Volleys look spectacular and are difficult to do.

STRANGER THINGS

In soccer, the basic terms are quite straightforward, but there are some very strange phrases. Here are a few of our favorites to add to your vocabulary.

JOURNEYMAN

A player who often changes club, never stopping at one for very long, as though they are on one long journey.

12TH MAN

You're only allowed 11 players on the field at one time, but if the crowd is being particularly loud and supportive, they can be described as the 12th man.

LOST THE LOCKER ROOM

Coaches give pep talks in the locker room. So if the players in a team no longer respect the coach, they have "lost the locker room."

FERGIE TIME

Sir Alex Ferguson (Fergie) was the manager of the world-famous UK club Manchester United for a long time and tended to get what he wanted, including more stoppage time than usual. If a referee gives lots of stoppage time, it is called Fergie time.

MAGIC SPONGE

A quite ordinary sponge used by physical therapists to treat injuries on the field. No one knows why or how it works, but we suspect it is magic.

FOX IN THE BOX

A player who is particularly effective in the penalty area. Dutch player Ruud van Nistelrooy was the foxiest in the box.

ONION BAG

Sometimes used to mean the goal because the netting looks sort of like a bag that onions come in.

GIANT KILLING

When a small, low-ranked team unexpectedly beats a strong, famous team.

PARK THE BUS

When all the players in a team play in defensive positions. It is as though they have parked a double-decker bus in front of the goalposts.

HOSPITAL PASS

A pass from your own player that puts you in danger of losing the ball.

HISTORY OF SOCCER

Soccer is a game that has changed a lot over time in all sorts of ways. We're going to go on a whistle-stop tour through the big moments in soccer history and find out how we got from playing with a ball made of feathers to using high-tech soccer balls. Find out when the rules and techniques we use now were invented, from the introduction of new formations to playing "Total Football." See how particular players, coaches, and clubs changed the way the game was played, from Cruyff to Herrera, Messi to Puskás, Sir Bobby Robson to Olympique Lyonnais Féminin.

Let's see the big moments that have changed the game.

PUSKÁS

W

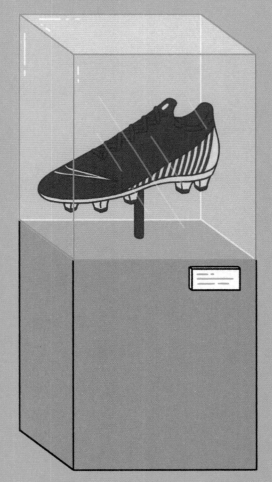

Soccer hasn't always been on TV and watched by millions of people. But people have played soccer, or something very similar, for thousands of years. Here's how it all began and how over time it has changed and evolved into what we watch and play today.

Early beginnings It all started in China, over 2,000 years ago with a game called "Ts'u-chü." The ball was made of leather, and it was stuffed with animal hair and feathers. The goal was as tall as five grown-ups stood on each other's heads and as narrow as a child. As you can imagine, with a goal this shape, it was incredibly difficult to score, and it was a very skillful game.

1925 The offside rule is changed so that only two opponents have to be between the attacker receiving the ball and the goal.

1920 On Boxing Day, Dick, Kerr Ladies beat St. Helen's Ladies 4–0 in a game watched by 53,000 inside the stadium, with many more outside the stadium trying to get in. The FA became jealous of the huge crowds that women's games were attracting, and in 1921, women's teams were banned from playing at men's club grounds. Thankfully, this ruling was overturned, but not until 1971. Now, whether you're a girl or boy, you can become a world-class soccer superstar. Soccer is for everyone.

1929 Serie A is formed in Italy.

1928 La Liga is formed in Spain with the first season starting a year later.

1930 The first FIFA World Cup took place in Uruguay. The home team beat Argentina 4–2 in the final to become the first ever world champions.

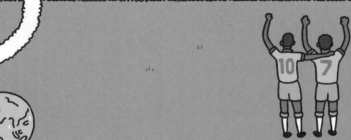

1920 Egypt become the first African team to play in a competitive international game, losing 2–1 to Italy at the Olympics in Belgium.

1951 The first white soccer ball is used in an official game, instead of a traditional brown ball.

1956 Real Madrid win the first ever European Cup. They would go on to win many more.

1958 Edson Arantes do Nascimento, aka Pelé, wins his first World Cup with Brazil along with teammate Mané Garrincha. Brazil never lost a game in which Pelé and Garrincha played together.

1969 The Women's FA was formed following an increase in the popularity of soccer after the 1966 World Cup.

2019 FIFA estimated one billion people tuned in globally to watch the Women's World Cup, breaking the record by a huge margin and signaling that the sport is getting the long-awaited attention it deserves.

2012 Lionel Messi scored 91 goals in a calendar year. That is, frankly, absurd. He might be an alien.

2010 The first World Cup to be hosted by an African nation was held in South Africa. Vuvuzelas (a type of horn) were blown by crowds and became iconic in the tournament.

2007 French team Olympique Lyonnais Féminin win the first of 13 consecutive league titles. They become the most dominant team in sports history.

1500s In Europe, the earliest examples of a game similar to soccer began in the 1500s in a city called Florence, which is now in Italy. The game was called "calcio" (pronounced "caltch-yo"). There was no limit on how many people could play at once. Instead of a field, players chased a ball all over town. It was so violent, and so many people got hurt in the chaos, that it was eventually banned.

1700s A similar game called "folk football" was played on the streets of London in the 1700s, but was also banned because of the serious injuries and damage it caused.

1862 The first professional club, Notts County, was formed, and in the following year, the Football Association (the FA) was born. This is when the game we know started to take shape.

1902 The penalty spot is invented. Before this, penalties were taken from anywhere along a line drawn 12 yards from the goal line.

1888 In 1888, the Football League was founded. The teams included Accrington, Aston Villa, Blackburn Rovers, Bolton Wanderers, Burnley, Derby County, Everton, Notts County, Preston North End, Stoke, West Bromwich Albion, and Wolverhampton Wanderers. The first league title was won by Preston, which went the whole season without losing a game.

1912 Goalkeepers can no longer handle the ball outside of the penalty area.

1900s

1971 The FA lift the ban on women playing at "men's" stadiums. The first ever women's FA Cup was held.

1991 China host the first Women's World Cup, with the USA overcoming Norway 2–1 in the final.

1992 The back pass rule is brought in. Goalkeepers are no longer allowed to pick up the ball with their hands if the ball is passed back to them by one of their own teammates, unless the ball is headed or chested to the goalie.

1970 Yellow and red cards are introduced.

2005 Liverpool were 3–0 down to A.C. Milan in the UEFA Champions League final in Istanbul. They pulled themselves together at halftime and came back to draw 3–3. Liverpool then won 3–2 on penalties. The game is known as the Miracle of Istanbul.

2002 Brazil won their fifth World Cup, making them the nation with the most World Cup wins.

2000 FIFA name Michelle Akers the Women's Player of the Century after winning two World Cups and one Olympic gold medal and pioneering the women's game.

1992 The Premier League is formed in England. The money in the game becomes huge.

2000s

1994 At the age of 42, Roger Milla becomes the oldest player ever to score at a World Cup at USA '94, and does a wiggly little dance at the corner flag to celebrate.

THE GREATEST TEAMS OF ALL TIME

Which is the greatest team of all time? This question causes arguments in playgrounds, at work, and at the dinner table in every country, every day. It's impossible to find a perfect answer. This list is not definitive, and you may find teams you prefer for various reasons, but without doubt, these teams all made history in their own amazing way.

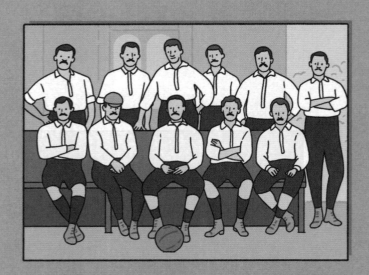

PRESTON NORTH END, UK
1888–89

This Preston North End team was invincible. They went a whole season without losing a single game. They did this 100 years before Arsène Wenger's Arsenal did in the Premier League in 2003–04.

In 1889, PNE won the league as well as the FA Cup, and managed not to concede a single goal in the tournament.

They didn't have one specific head coach, but instead had a committee whose job it was to select the players. PNE played in a 2-3-5 formation, which was popular at the time, and used their players very well.

DICK, KERR LADIES, UK
1917–25

During World War I, at the Preston branch of a locomotive and tramcar manufacturer called Dick, Kerr & Co., female employees started playing in their breaks, and they became incredibly good.

In 1917, Dick, Kerr Ladies played the factory's men's team and won. In 1920, they played against St. Helen's Ladies in front of 53,000 people.

In 1922, Dick, Kerr Ladies toured North America. They played nine men's teams, winning three games and drawing three. The men's teams included professional players and future USA national team players.

HUNGARY NATIONAL TEAM
1950–56

Also known as the Mighty Magyars or the Golden Team, the Hungary national team played 50 games over six years and lost only one of them, to West Germany in the 1954 World Cup final.

They were coached by Gusztáv Sebes, and their best player was Ferenc Puskás. The Puskás Award for the most impressive goal of the season in world soccer is named after him.

The Magyars won gold in the 1952 Olympics and beat England 6–3 at Wembley in what became known as the Match of the Century a year later. They scored in 73 consecutive games, which is still a record. The Golden Team indeed!

REAL MADRID, SPAIN
1955–60

This Real Madrid team was the original Galácticos (superstars). There were stars in every position on the field, but the best were Francisco Gento (left wing), Raymond Kopa (right wing), Alfredo Di Stéfano (center forward), and Ferenc Puskás (center forward or inside forward).

The legendary Di Stéfano would often drop back into the midfield, which meant that this Real Madrid side could switch easily from a 3-2-5 formation to a 3-2-2-3 formation, which was confusing to their opponents!

The original Galácticos won five European Cups (Champions Leagues) in a row. This had never been done before and has never been done since.

AJAX, NETHERLANDS
1970-73

This Ajax side was coached by Rinus Michels, who became a very influential soccer manager. In 1970, Michels taught his players about Total Football. He wanted every player to be able to play every position, so if you noticed your teammate was out of position, you would be able to step in.

Ajax was close to relegation when Michels took over, but he turned them into champions.

Michels left for Barcelona in 1971 and was replaced by Stefán Kovács. It was down to Kovács and Ajax hero Johan Cruyff that they won three European Cups in a row.

GERMANY WOMEN'S NATIONAL TEAM
1989-2008

This was one of the most successful international soccer teams of all time. In German, they are called the Deutsche Fußballnationalmannschaft der Frauen, and they had a winning spree between their first European Championships win in 1989 and their World Cup win in 2007.

They have won eight of the 12 European Championships so far, and claimed six consecutive titles between 1995 and 2013. They also won the World Cup in 2003 and claimed Olympic bronze in 2000, 2004, and 2008. Superstar Birgit Prinz scored 128 goals in 214 appearances. It is fair to say they have won the lot.

BARCELONA 2008-11
& SPAIN 2008-12

These two sides played a style of soccer called tiki-taka. This is a technique where players make lots of little passes without letting the other side touch the ball. These teams shared many of the same players and dominated European soccer for four years.

Barcelona was so good at keeping the ball that if you wanted to touch the ball when you were up against them, it was probably just better to bring your own ball from home and do kick-ups in the corner until the game was over.

For those four years, it seemed as though players such as Messi, Xavi, Iniesta, and Busquets could not be beaten, until the rest of the world figured out how to play in the same way.

Spain won the Euros in 2008 and 2012, and the World Cup in 2010. Barcelona won La Liga in 2009, 2010, and 2011, as well as the treble in 2009 of La Liga, Copa del Rey, and Champions League. Barcelona won the Champions League again in 2011 and is considered by many to be the greatest soccer team of all time.

OLYMPIQUE LYONNAIS FÉMININ, FRANCE
2007–19

Lyon's women's team is the most dominant soccer team of all time. With star players such as England's Lucy Bronze, Wendie Renard, Amandine Henry, legendary striker Eugénie Le Sommer, and the Ballon d'Or–winning Ada Hegerberg, Lyon has been simply amazing.

Since 2010, Lyon has won six Champions League titles, four of them coming consecutively between 2016 and 2019, as well as 13 consecutive French Ligue 1s from 2007 to 2019. This sort of domination may never be seen again in soccer anywhere in the world.

REAL MADRID, SPAIN
2016-18

With Madrid hero Zinedine Zidane, nicknamed "Zizou," as the coach, the team won three Champions Leagues in a row, something that hadn't happened for over 40 years.

Zizou took over from Rafa Benítez at Real Madrid in 2016. This was controversial, as Rafa had only lost three games in his time as coach. However, Zizou went on to dominate the Champions League with Real Madrid just as he had done as a player. If anyone was going to get the best out of Real Madrid's megastars, it makes sense that it was Zizou, the ultimate Galáctico.

USA WOMEN'S NATIONAL TEAM
1991-PRESENT

Since winning that first World Cup in 1991, the USA went on to win the competition again in 1999, 2015, and 2019. Alongside the World Cup success came Olympic gold medals in 1996, 2004, 2008, and 2012. That's a lot of trophies and gold medals. They've won the CONCACAF Cup eight times, the Algarve Cup ten times, and two of the first four She Believes Cups since it began in 2016. They have been unstoppable.

Many of the greatest women ever to play the game have represented the USA, including their top three goalscorers of all time: Abby Wambach (184 goals), Mia Hamm (158 goals), and Kristine Lilly (130 goals).

SOCCER CLEATS PAST TO PRESENT

Do you have a favorite pair of soccer cleats? Nowadays, soccer cleats are super-high-tech tools, every tiny detail designed to help players run and kick perfectly and, of course, to look cool. It took a long time to get to this point. The amazing Predators or Vapors you have on your feet today are very different from the soggy leather clogs that our soccer ancestors were wearing. Let's take a look at the evolution of the cleat...

1800s

In the 1800s, if you wanted to play soccer, you played in your work boots. They were thick, heavy leather boots. The leather went up past your ankles, and in the rain, they could weigh more than two pounds. They often had steel toecaps. Imagine getting a steel kick in a tackle. Ouch!

1990s

The 1990s saw the release of the iconic adidas Predators. Predators had rubber ridges where you were most likely to strike the ball, helping you to "grip" it and add curve to your shots. Predators have evolved over time to the ultra-high-tech-engineered version we see now. Zidane scored one of the greatest goals of all time in the 2002 Champions League final wearing Predator Manias.

1994

Nike brought out the Tiempo Premiers for the 1994 World Cup in the USA. The Nike Tiempo has been a popular cleat since then, with players such as Ronaldinho, Andrea Pirlo, and Francesco Totti all being extremely good at soccer while wearing them.

1998

Nike created the Mercurial cleat in 1998. They were silver, blue, yellow, and swirly. They were lighter than most cleats. Ronaldo had a special pair that Nike called the "R9s." In 2002, the Mercurials evolved into the timeless Mercurial Vapors.

Thierry Daniel Henry was a forward who played for Monaco, Juventus, Barcelona, the New York Red Bulls, and, most famously, Arsenal. Premier League defenses were used to dealing with powerful forwards who acted as target men. Henry caused havoc in his Mercurial Vapors.

1954

In 1954, a German named Adi Dassler created a new type of soccer cleat. You guessed it; this was the beginning of adidas. Adi Dassler designed screw-in studs that could be attached to your shoes, giving you better grip on rainy, muddy surfaces.

1970s

In the 1970s, Alan Ball became the first player to wear white shoes. Ball was famous for winning the World Cup with England in 1966. His shoes were designed by Hummel, and they were so bright that the commentator called him "Twinkle Toes."

1980s

Puma released the Puma King in the 1980s, and they became a competitor to the Copa Mundial. Puma Kings were worn by players such as Diego Maradona and Johan Cruyff, while Alan Shearer scored hundreds of goals in the new Umbro cleats.

1979

In 1979, adidas released the Copa Mundial. They had big tongues to cover the laces. Tongues were popular because covering the laces was thought to help players strike more accurately. The Copa Mundials were simple, durable, and comfy. They are the best-selling cleat of all time.

2010

The 2010s saw a return to the ankle collar. This time they were for comfort rather than protection. Modern cleats are also often laceless to help shooting accuracy. No fancy cleat helps as much as simply practicing a lot. Modern cleats are amazing, but striker Sergio Agüero could play in rain boots and he'd still score goals for fun.

Jackie Milburn is a Newcastle United legend who complained that the new cleats were too light. Jackie wanted heavy, durable cleats. He would wear his sturdy soccer cleats in the bath, or when he was working in the mines, so that they would mold to his feet.

Blades started to replace studs in the late '90s, as they provided better grip. But, by the end of the '00s, they'd dipped in popularity as they gave so much grip on the field that players began twisting their ankles and complaining of injuries.

THE EVOLUTION OF THE BALL

The ball. The most important thing of all! Without the soccer ball, there'd be no last-minute wonder goals, no last-ditch headers, no...well, nothing really. The ball has changed a lot from its humble beginnings as anything sort-of round to the sleek and perfected ball we have now.

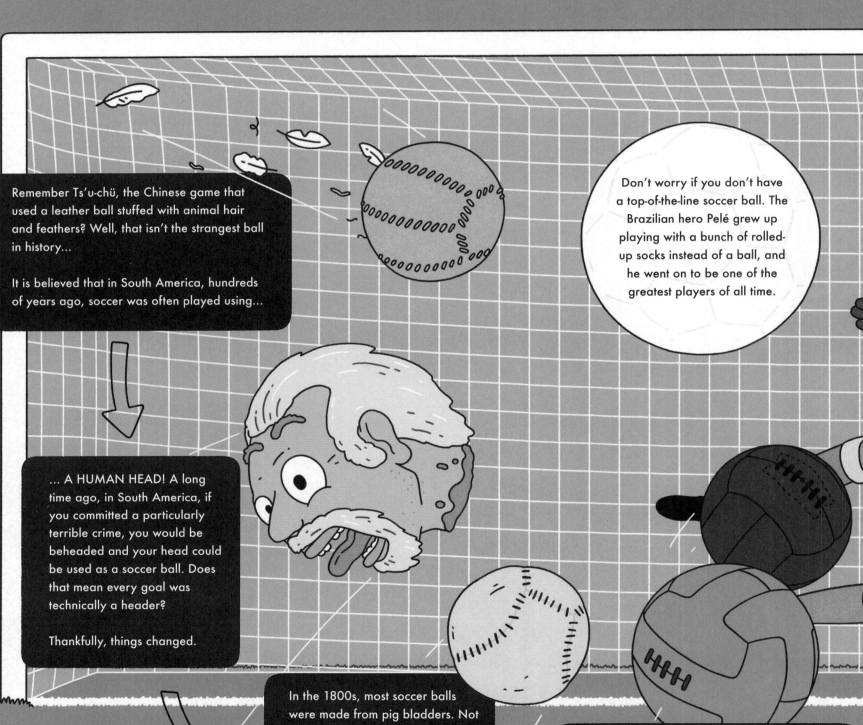

Remember Ts'u-chü, the Chinese game that used a leather ball stuffed with animal hair and feathers? Well, that isn't the strangest ball in history...

It is believed that in South America, hundreds of years ago, soccer was often played using...

Don't worry if you don't have a top-of-the-line soccer ball. The Brazilian hero Pelé grew up playing with a bunch of rolled-up socks instead of a ball, and he went on to be one of the greatest players of all time.

... A HUMAN HEAD! A long time ago, in South America, if you committed a particularly terrible crime, you would be beheaded and your head could be used as a soccer ball. Does that mean every goal was technically a header?

Thankfully, things changed.

In the 1800s, most soccer balls were made from pig bladders. Not all pig bladders are the same size, which meant neither were soccer balls. It was in the late 1800s when the FA decided that all balls used in their competitions must be roughly the same size and weight. This meant that a new way of making soccer balls had to be found.

In the first official World Cup Final between Uruguay and Argentina in 1930, both teams used their own soccer balls instead of a neutral ball provided by FIFA. In the first half, Argentina used their own soccer ball, and they were 2–1 up at halftime. Uruguay used their ball in the second half and went on to win the game 4–2.

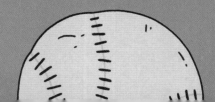

The ball used for the 2018 World Cup in Russia was a modern version of the adidas Telstar. It was black and white, just like the original Telstar.

Benjamin Pavard scored the best goal of the 2018 World Cup with the adidas Telstar 18. It was a totally ridiculous, rising volley from outside the area. France were losing 2–1 at the time, and went on to win 4–3.

At the 2010 World Cup, the Jabulani ball was released. It had just eight panels, which made it incredibly smooth. This made the ball move around unpredictably in the air. Strikers and goalkeepers complained, as nobody knew what was going to happen to the ball after it had been kicked. It was chaotic, but very exciting.

For the 2006 World Cup in Germany, adidas introduced the Teamgeist soccer ball. It had 14 panels instead of the 32 in the Buckminster design. This made it smoother and more streamlined. Being streamlined means that the shape of something helps it to move faster through the air.

The first non-black-and-white official ball was used at the 1998 World Cup in France. The ball was white with blue and red details— the same colors as the French flag—and was named the Tricolore.

In 1951, the first ever white-and-orange soccer balls were allowed in competitive games, to aid visibility in bad weather. Previously, all balls were brown.

In 1970, the first official World Cup ball was produced: the adidas Telstar. This is what most people imagine when they think of a soccer ball. The black-and-white design was created by Richard Buckminster Fuller and is called the Buckminster Design.

BRAZIL 1970 WORLD CUP FINAL GOAL

Brazilian right wingback Carlos Alberto scored one of the greatest World Cup goals ever with the adidas Telstar in the 1970 final against Italy. Pelé set him up. Nice.

THE GREAT PLAYERS

From year to year, season to season, week to week, and even from day to day, different players fall in and out of favor for all sorts of reasons. It can seem impossible to keep up. However, there are some players from history who are indisputable legends. Players who were heads, shoulders, knees, and toes above everyone else playing around them. We've chosen 11 of the greatest for you to read about, dream about, and learn from.

BORN: June 26, 1968, Milan, Italy

PLAYED FOR: 906 appearances for A.C. Milan between 1984 and 2009, 126 appearances for Italy.

WHAT THEY SAID ABOUT PAOLO: Italian striker Alessandro Del Piero said, "There are great players and there are world-class players. Then there are those who manage to go beyond that term. Paolo is the perfect example."

FACT: His dad, Cesare, also played for A.C. Milan and also won the Champions League with them as captain, 40 years before Paolo did.

Maldini was a magnificent defender because he could do everything. He was a dogged marker, a graceful passer, an elegant dribbler, a fantastic crosser, and a precise tackler. He was a very intelligent player with unrivaled tactical awareness and knowledge. He also taught himself to kick equally well with either foot.

All of this meant that Maldini could play in any defensive position: left, right, center, wingback, wherever. With A.C. Milan, he won 7 Serie A titles and 5 Champions Leagues. He won the lot, did Paolo, and had gorgeous hair to go with it.

PAOLO MALDINI
DEFENDER

GOALKEEPER

LEV YASHIN

BORN: October 22, 1929, Moscow, Russia

PLAYED FOR: 326 appearances for Dynamo Moscow from 1950 to 1970, 74 appearances for the Soviet Union.

WHAT THEY SAID ABOUT LEV: Portuguese legend Eusebio called him "the peerless goalkeeper of the century."

FACT: Also played international ice hockey. He was a goalkeeper in this sport, too.

Lev Yashin was born in the Soviet Union (now Russia) and was in their World Cup squad four times. He was known as "the Black Spider" because of his uniform and because he made so many saves it was as though he had eight legs.

His clothes weren't actually black, they were dark blue, but on the black-and-white TVs of the time, his clothes looked black to the people watching.

He was incredibly acrobatic and had a reputation for putting strikers off just by being so scary. He saved 150 penalties and kept 270 clean sheets and is the only goalkeeper ever to win the Ballon d'Or (the award for the best player in the world).

DEFENDER
JOY FAWCETT

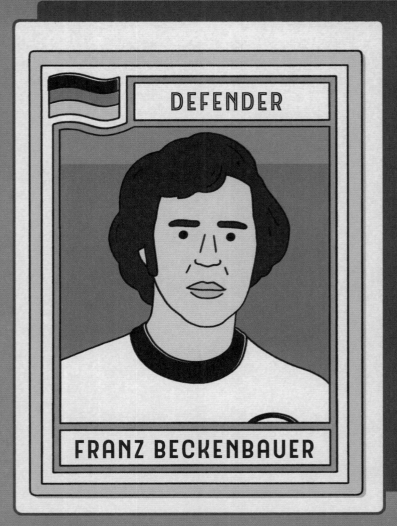

DEFENDER

FRANZ BECKENBAUER

BORN: February 8, 1968, California, USA

PLAYED FOR: 43 appearances for San Diego Spirit, 241 appearances for USA national team between 1987 and 2004.

WHAT THEY SAID ABOUT JOY: The USA Women's Team Hall of Fame said, "Her innate ability to read the game, to defuse potential danger before it became dangerous, was one of her greatest and always overlooked talents."

FACT: Currently assistant coach for USA Women's Deaf Team.

Fawcett was tenacious, tough, and extremely smart. She won the first ever Women's World Cup with the USA in China in 1991, and went on to win 241 caps for the USA.

She had children while she was still a player, came back to the sport immediately after they were born, and played as if she'd never been away. Having a baby is probably one of the most difficult things a human can do, but Fawcett did it and then just immediately started giving opposition attackers nightmares again. She then went on to become a founding member of the WUSA.

BORN: September 11, 1945, Munich, Germany

PLAYED FOR: 439 appearances for Bayern Munich, 105 for New York Cosmos, 28 for Hamburger SV, 103 for West Germany.

WHAT THEY SAID ABOUT FRANZ: Brian Clough, European Cup-winning manager with Nottingham Forest, remembered that he "once saw Franz Beckenbauer enter a restaurant and he did it the same way he played football: with class and authority."

FACT: The first player to win the World Cup, European Championships, and European Cup (Champions League) all as captain.

Franz Beckenbauer invented a position. Beckenbauer was the first attacking sweeper, or libero. He was a rock-solid defender, but he was also very comfortable on the ball. He would win the ball back from the opposition, then run with it all the way to the other end of the field and create attacking opportunities for his team. He did the job of three or four players on his own.

He was known as Der Kaiser, which means "the Emperor" in German.

JOHAN CRUYFF

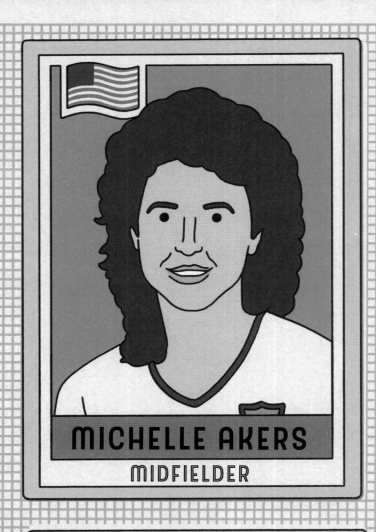

MIDFIELDER

BORN: April 25, 1947, Amsterdam, Netherlands

PLAYED FOR: 273 appearances for Ajax, 143 for Barcelona, 23 for Los Angeles Aztecs, 30 for Washington Diplomats, 10 for Levante, 33 for Feyenoord.

WHAT THEY SAID ABOUT JOHAN: Dutch player Johan Neeskens said, "If you look at the greatest players in history, most of them couldn't coach. If you look at the greatest coaches in history, most of them were not great players. Johan Cruyff did both—and in such an exhilarating style."

FACT: He invented a whole style of soccer called "Total Football."

Johan Cruyff is labeled as a midfielder here, but he could play in any position (except maybe goalkeeper).

Cruyff was a huge believer in "Total Football," which is the idea that every outfield player on the field should be able to

---

BORN: February 1, 1966, California, USA

PLAYED FOR: Tyresö FF, Orlando Lions Women, 155 appearances for the USA national team between 1985 and 200.

WHAT THEY SAID ABOUT MICHELLE: Mia Hamm, fellow USA national team player, said, "If it's a header, I'm putting all my money, and all the other team's money, on Michelle."

FACT: She started playing as a striker, and was probably the best player in the world. She scored in almost every game she played. She won the Golden Boot for most goals scored at the 1991 World Cup in China, and won with the USA.

After the World Cup, she started feeling constantly exhausted and was told she had chronic fatigue and immune dysfunction syndrome, which made her feel tired all the time.

She could have stopped playing after that, but she didn't. She played as a defensive midfielder instead, a position in which she didn't need to sprint as much.

She went on to win the World Cup again with the USA in 1999. All hail Queen Akers!

MICHELLE AKERS
MIDFIELDER

play in every position. So if he noticed that a right-back player went

sprinting up the field to help the attack, he would just fill in the space the right back had left while somebody else filled his position and so on. (Read more about positions on p. 34.)

Cruyff won eight Eredivisie (the top Dutch League) titles with Ajax. He played in this Total Football style at Barcelona, too. In 1974 he helped Barcelona to win their first Liga (the top Spanish League) since 1960. He won three Ballons d'Or and helped to change the way soccer is played.

Cruyff also invented an astonishing and signature move called the Cruyff Turn. He would feign a pass mid-dribble and then turn and speed off in the opposite direction. Pep Guardiola was a student of Johan Cruyff and shares a lot of the same tactical ideas.

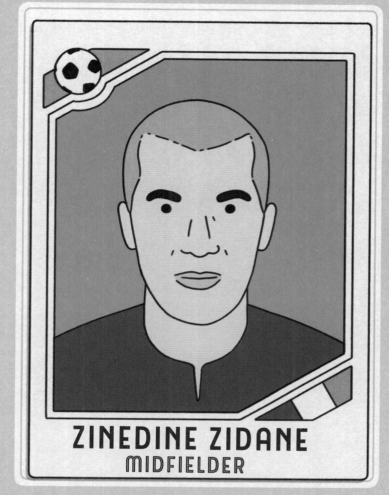

ZINEDINE ZIDANE
MIDFIELDER

BORN: June 23, 1972, Marseille, France

PLAYED FOR: 61 appearances for Cannes, 139 for Bordeaux, 151 for Juventus, 155 for Real Madrid, 108 for France.

WHAT THEY SAID ABOUT ZIZOU: Zlatan Ibrahimović said, "When Zidane stepped onto the pitch, the 10 other guys just got suddenly better. It was magic. He was a unique player. He was more than good, he came from another planet. His teammates became like him when he was on the pitch."

FACT: Got sent off in the 2010 World Cup final, his last ever game.

Known by his teammates as Zizou, he moved around the field like a dancer, with elegance and grace. He could shoot equally well with either foot, and he was the master of the "roulette," a skill move that involves spinning past your opponent like a ballet dancer.

He scored one of the greatest ever Champions League goals for Real Madrid in the final against Leverkusen in 2002. The ball was hooked high into the sky by Roberto Carlos, and as it fell, Zizou never took his eyes off it, opened up his body, and smashed a volley into the top corner with his ever-so-slightly weaker left foot. Zizou won the Italian Serie A twice, La Liga once, the Champions League once, and the World Cup in France. He scored two headers in the World Cup final in 1998 with his lovely, shiny skull.

SIR STANLEY MATTHEWS
MIDFIELDER

MARTA VIEIRA DA SILVA
ATTACKER

BORN: February 1, 1915, Stoke-on-Trent, UK

PLAYED FOR: 355 appearances for Stoke City, 428 for Blackpool, 54 for England.

WHAT THEY SAID ABOUT STANLEY: Gianfranco Zola, a former Chelsea and Italy player, said, "Stanley told me he used to play for just £20 a week. Today he would be worth all the money in the Bank of England."

FACT: Despite the horrendous apartheid laws (which meant black people were not given the same rights as white people) in place in South Africa at the time, Stanley Matthews traveled to Soweto in 1975 and set up an all-black youth team in the area. He coached young South Africans of all races for years afterward.

Known as "the Wizard of the Dribble," Matthews played as a winger and ran with the ball unlike anybody else at the time. He won the first ever Ballon d'Or in 1956, and was so fit that he played until he was 50 years old in the top division in England, which is a record to this day. Matthews won the FA Cup with Blackpool in 1953.

BORN: February 19, 1986, Alagoas, Brazil

PLAYED FOR: 16 appearances at Vasco da Gama, 103 for Umeå IK, 24 for FC Gold Pride, 49 for Orlando Pride, 147 for Brazil.

WHAT MARTA SAID: After being knocked out of the World Cup in 2019, Marta said, "The women's game depends on you to survive. So think about that. Value it more. Cry in the beginning so you can smile in the end."

FACT: Her 17 goals at World Cup finals cemented her position as top World Cup goal scorer of all time.

Marta is often referred to as the greatest female soccer player of all time, and with good reason. Her dribbling skills are second to none.

She's incredibly fast and has scored an impressive number of goals despite not always playing as a striker.

BORN: October 23, 1940, Minas Gerais, Brazil

PLAYED FOR: 656 (1,120 including friendlies) appearances for Santos, 107 for NY Cosmos, 92 for Brazil.

WHAT THEY SAID ABOUT PELÉ: Former Manchester United striker Eric Cantona said that Pelé was "an artist in my eyes, someone who can lighten up a dark room."

FACT: As a child, Pele used to practice with a newspaper rolled up into a ball with a piece of string attached to it.

For a long time, Pelé was considered to be the greatest soccer player of all time, and he still is by some. He played as a striker or as an attacking midfielder and had many fantastic skills, but his main talent was scoring goals. Pelé scored 1,283 goals in 1,366 games.

Pelé was named the FIFA Player of the Century for the 20th Century. He won three World Cups with Brazil and two Copa Libertadores with Santos.

EDSON ARANTES DO NASCIMENTO

AKA **PELÉ**

ATTACKER

37

LIONEL MESSI

...ACKER

BORN: June 24, 1987, Rosario, Argentina

PLAYED FOR: Newell's Old Boys before moving to Barcelona, for whom he has made 687 appearances.

WHAT THEY SAID ABOUT MESSI: Ex-teammate at Barcelona Javier Mascherano said, "Although he may not be human, it's good that Messi still thinks he is."

Messi plays soccer at a different level from everyone else. He is arguably the greatest soccer player there has ever been. He is one of the most impressive finishers, passers, free-kick takers, and dribblers of all time. He also has a sixth sense when it comes to the sport. He knows the perfect place to stand, exactly when to run, the right moment to pass, and the precise angle at which to shoot. Sometimes skill like this can't be taught and instead it should just be admired.

LEGENDARY COACHES
AND HOW THEY DID IT

Coaching soccer is difficult. Imagine having to tell 11 people on a big field where to stand while you have a bench of subs next to you who all think they should be playing, and 50,000 people in a crowd who, really, think they should be playing too. But it's also super rewarding. Winning trophies for your players, your club, and your fans must be the most amazing feeling in the world. And to do so you have to be pretty smart. Not in a way that means you finish top in the class at everything, just in a way that means you have your own ideas and act on them. And when your own ideas are not going well, you are flexible enough to change them.

Here are those coaches who changed the way soccer was played forever, and some examples of the formations they played and why.

THE KEY POSITIONS

Where you play on the field is not just random. You probably have something you are particularly good at: maybe you run fast, maybe you are tall, maybe you like to think up clever tactics, and maybe you have a knack for smashing in goals. Whatever it is, there is a position for you. The job of a coach or manager is to choose which players they think will work best in which position and match their special skills to work well with the rest of the team. Here are the key positions as well as some slightly more specialist ones.

GOALKEEPER

The goalie is the only player allowed to use their hands, and with that comes a lot of responsibility. Their main job is to stop the ball from going into the net. They need good concentration, to be agile, to have good reactions, and increasingly, they need to be able to pass the ball well.

FULLBACK

There are usually two fullback players, a left back and a right back. They go on the sides of the defense, on either side of the center backs. They need to be quick and good at changing direction, as opposition "wingers" will try to dribble past them to get closer to the penalty area, or to the edge of the area to put in a cross. Increasingly, fullbacks are often expected to link up attacks and even score goals themselves.

CENTER BACK

The center back, sometimes known as a center half, is the player in the middle of the defense. Their main job is to stop the opposition from getting any chances to have a shot at a goal. They're usually big—normally the biggest on the field. They also have to be strong, be able to read the game, be able to intercept opposition passes and predict them before they happen, and also be very brave.

CENTER MIDFIELD

Often referred to as the "Engine of the Team," a center midfielder needs many qualities. They're in the middle of the field and will need to be able to win headers and tackles, make interceptions, start attacks, play long balls, and indeed score goals. They are busy bees.

STRIKER

The striker's main job is to score goals. Strikers come in all shapes and sizes, but generally have one outstanding quality: they are good at finishing.

DEFENSIVE MIDFIELD

Similar to the center midfielder, but the defensive midfielder plays deeper, just in front of the defense. Claude Makélélé was possibly the best ever at this: identifying attacks and stopping them before they could get going. In fact, he was so good that people often refer to this position as the "Makélélé" role.

WINGER

The winger's job is to create and score goals, usually by starting wide and taking on the opposition's fullback with skill and pace. Traditionally, a winger would get to the bye-line and put in a cross, but a winger's job has evolved more to getting into the penalty area, cutting in, and scoring goals themselves.

WINGBACK

A wingback will usually play in a "Back Five": a formation that has three center backs and two wingbacks. They play down the sides—the wings—of the field, like a fullback, but are expected to move up and down the field more. They have to be amazingly fit to do this.

TREQUARTISTA OR NUMBER 10

They play ahead of the midfield but behind the strikers. They are imaginative and skillful—Argentinian Diego Maradona could be considered a trequartista.

LIBERO OR SWEEPER

They go behind the two center backs and sweep up the danger. They are strong and can read the game like a book.

UTILITY PLAYER

A player who doesn't have a specific position and can slot in where necessary. James Milner is a good example: he's great all over the field.

COACHES AND FORMATIONS

Most teams who win anything have a good coach, or manager, behind them. Lots of coaches are reliable and effective, but some are absolute game changers in the truest sense of the word. They invent formations, which means they plan where each player is positioned on the field. Formations are often a coach's trademark and key to their success. Here are a few of the best, along with their favorite killer formations and most innovative tactics.

RINUS MICHELS

Marinus Jacobus Hendricus Michels is the wise owl of soccer coaches. Michels invented the version of "Total Football" that is commonly referred to in modern soccer. You don't get named FIFA Coach of the Century for nothing. He inspired many coaches who followed, including Johan Cruyff and Pep Guardiola, who you are about to meet.

As a coach, Michels won the European Cup, the European Championship, four Eredivisies, three KNVB Cups, La Liga, and the Copa del Rey.

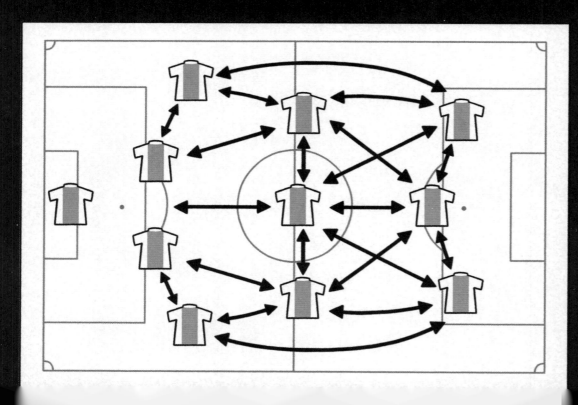

TOTAL FOOTBALL

Every player in the team should be capable of playing any position on the field.

Players have to be very versatile and responsive. Only versatile players can play Total Football.

If a player leaves their position, another player takes up the empty space so that all the positions are covered at any given time. Pep Guardiola's Manchester City does this well.

The lineage of Total Football is traceable throughout time. Michels coached Cruyff and Cruyff coached Guardiola.

JOHAN CRUYFF

Johan Cruyff is thought to be the most influential man in soccer from the past 50 years, if not of all time. He was coached by Michels and took Total Football even further.

Cruyff made sure that the youth, reserve, and first teams at his clubs played the same tactics so that it was easier to promote youth players to the first team. He created the training exercise called "rondos." Rondos is a bit like monkey-in-the-middle with a soccer. It helps develop players' spatial awareness.

Ajax's youth academy is based on Cruyff's soccer philosophy. He also helped to establish the famous Barcelona youth academy, La Masia. La Masia teaches players to be humble and unselfish so that they can learn more. Many of the best players of the past two decades were educated at La Masia. In 2012, Barcelona played a team made up entirely of La Masia graduates: Víctor Valdés, Jordi Alba, Carles Puyol, Gerard Piqué, Martín Montoya, Sergio Busquets, Xavi, Andrés Iniesta, Cesc Fàbregas, Pedro and Lionel Messi.

Cruyff's Barcelona won La Liga four times in a row, as well as the 1992 Champions League, after which a million people lined the streets of Barcelona to celebrate their return. Cruyff is also famous for having fantastic hair.

PEP GUARDIOLA

Josep "Pep" Guardiola played under the management of Johan Cruyff and Bobby Robson at Barcelona.

In his first season as Barcelona coach, he won the first ever treble in Spanish soccer and became the youngest coach to win the Champions League.

Pep and Manchester City became the first coach and team to earn 100 points in a Premier League season and the first English men's team to complete a domestic treble (FA Cup, League Cup, and Premier League).

Pep invented a formation tactic called "the false 9." He instructed Lionel Messi to play in the center of the attack, but also to drop deep and look for the ball. Guardiola is also responsible for making goalkeepers more comfortable on the ball. This is because his tactics require goalkeepers to play the ball out from the back and act as an extra outfield player.

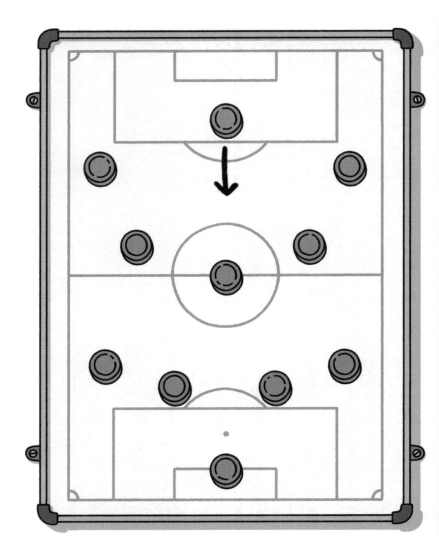

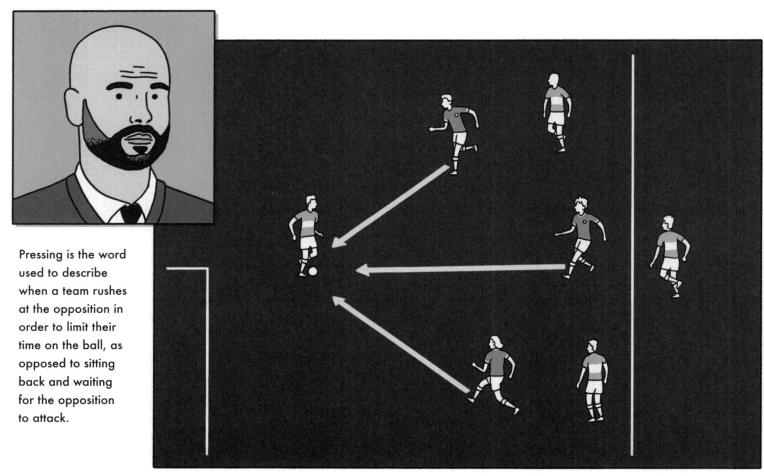

Pressing is the word used to describe when a team rushes at the opposition in order to limit their time on the ball, as opposed to sitting back and waiting for the opposition to attack.

VALERIY LOBANOVSKYI

Not all coaches make it big through formations and tactics alone. Lobanovskyi was one of the first coaches to place importance on the fitness and diet of his players.

He won the second most trophies of any coach ever, after Alex Ferguson, winning 13 league titles in Ukraine and the Soviet Union, nine cups in the same countries, two Cup Winners Cups, and one European Super Cup.

He also managed to steer Dynamo Kyiv to the semifinals of the 1999 Champions League among some incredible competition from English, Spanish, German, and Italian sides.

BOB PAISLEY

Bob Paisley was born in Hetton-le-Hole, played for Bishop Auckland, and then made the move directly to Liverpool, which is quite a jump. As a manager, Bob was given the task of following the legendary Bill Shankly, who had become a hero at Anfield (Liverpool's stadium).

Paisley was in charge of Liverpool for nine years, winning nothing in his first year. After that first year, though, he won at least one major trophy in every year of his time at Liverpool, including six league titles, three European Cups, and the UEFA Cup! Only two other managers have won three Champions Leagues: Zinedine Zidane and Carlo Ancelotti.

Paisley's teams would mainly play a 4-4-2 formation. This was one of the most popular formations for most of the 1980s and is still used by many teams today. Two lines of four players in midfield and defense is difficult to break down, while counter-attacking is made possible with two central strikers forming a partnership.

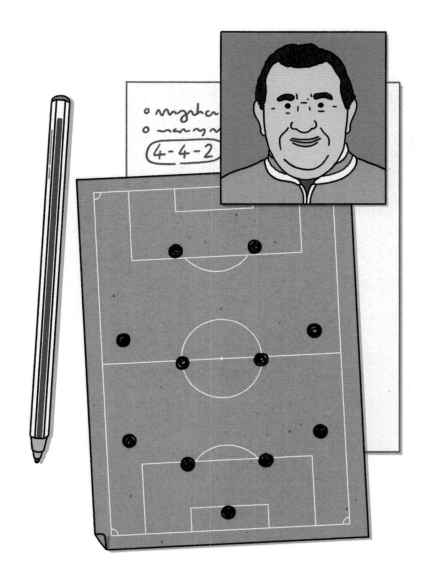

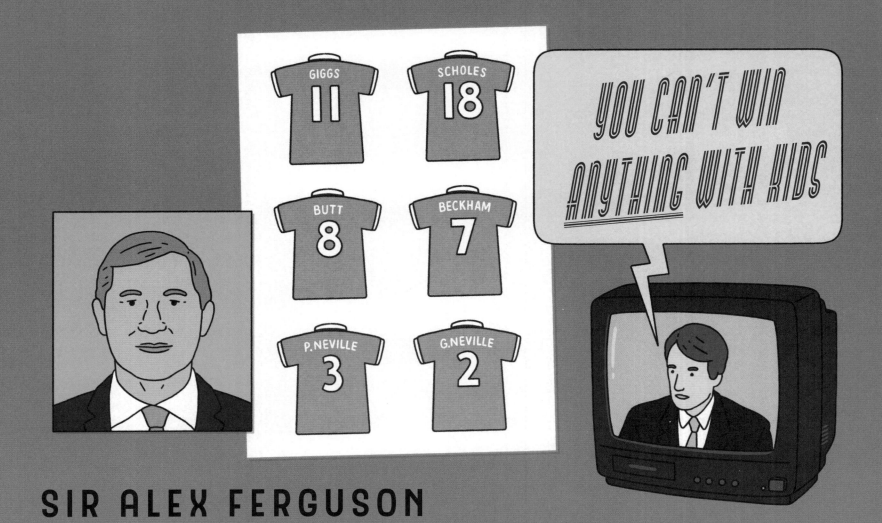

SIR ALEX FERGUSON

Sir Alexander Chapman Ferguson, or Fergie, is the most successful Manchester United manager. At the young age of 32, he started his coaching career at East Stirlingshire, with whom he started winning league titles.

He moved to Manchester United in 1986. It took him until 1993 to win the league, although he did win the FA Cup and the League Cup in the meantime. When three of United's best players, Hughes, Ince, and Kanchelskis, left the club in 1995, people lost confidence in Fergie. He chose six very young inexperienced players from the youth setup. They were Gary and Phil Neville, David Beckham, Nicky Butt, Paul Scholes, and Ryan Giggs. They all turned out to be superstars and became known as the class of '92. Sir Alex coined the phrase "squeaky bum time," meaning when things get tense toward the end of a game or season.

Sir Alex liked a few different formations, including 4-2-3-1. In this formation, the midfield is very full. This means that the opponents find it hard to command space in the middle and may have to resort to playing risky long balls.

CORINNE DIACRE

Corinne Diacre began her career as a defender. She played for the French national side, making 121 appearances. In August 2014, Diacre became the first woman to manage a men's soccer team, Clermont Foot. This was a huge step for women in the sport and a testament to her sheer tactical brilliance and insight in the sport.

She is now the coach of the French women's national team, which features many players from the very successful Lyon squad.

CHAN YUEN TING

Chan Yuen Ting was born in Hong Kong in 1988. In 2016, she won the Hong Kong Premier League as coach of the men's team, Eastern Sports Club.

It is very rare for a professional coach or manager to be this young because it can be difficult to lead a team where most of the players are older. Chan Yuen Ting did not let this faze her and took her men's team to victory, winning in Hong Kong's top division when she was only 27. She became the first female soccer coach to win a men's top division in international history. She has helped to increase the popularity of the Hong Kong Premier League.

Her favorite formation is 4-3-3, which is one of the most popular formations in soccer right now. It was used by the famous Dutch, Ajax, and Barcelona teams that played Total Football.

THE BIG CUPS

Across the world, in every country there are soccer leagues of every quality. A league is a set of teams of a similar standard. Within a season, each team within a league will play every other team a certain number of times (usually twice: home and away). Each game has points ascribed to it, and the team that wins the most points on the league table wins the league.

A cup competition is slightly different from a league. Cup competitions usually involve knock-out games, meaning that if a team loses, they leave the competition. Occasionally there are group stages to a cup competition, which means there are mini leagues, followed by a knock-out final stage.

The international cups are arguably the most dramatic competitions. They tend to be the biggest, most watched, and most special to the teams that win them.

WORLD CUP (MEN'S)

To a soccer fan, the World Cup is like a birthday, but if a birthday came around every four years and lasted for a whole month. It's the biggest, most exciting, most colorful festival of sports in the world. It features the best national teams from around the world, and for the month that it runs, the entire globe seems to catch soccer fever.

Started by a man named Jules Rimet, the first World Cup took place in 1930 in Uruguay. Thirteen teams took part and Uruguay were victorious. Since then, seven other countries have won titles: Brazil has five (1958, 1962, 1970, 1994, 2002), Italy have four (1934, 1938, 1982, 2006), Germany has four (1954, 1974, 1990, 2014), Argentina has two (1978, 1986), France has two (1998, 2018), England has one (1966), and Spain has one (2010). Uruguay won once more in 1950, when they beat the host country Brazil, at the Estádio do Maracanã in Rio de Janeiro, 2–1. Over 199,000 watched the nail-biter of a game.

One of the most famous goals was scored at the Mexico 1986 World Cup. Diego Maradona headed in an unlikely and impressive goal for Argentina against England that some people felt was a handball. When interviewed about it, he said he had scored it "a little with my head, and a little with the hand of God." Argentina went on to win the cup.

WORLD CUP (WOMEN'S)

Historically, women's soccer has not been given the attention it deserves. The Women's World Cup didn't officially start until 1991, 61 years after the men's. The first tournament was officially called the FIFA World Championship for Women's Football for the M&M's Cup. The United States won it, and their star player, Michelle Akers was the top scorer with ten goals. That's four more goals than Harry Kane scored at the 2018 World Cup!

The USA has won the World Cup four times, Germany has won it twice, and Japan and Norway have won one each.

At the 2019 World Cup in France, legendary Brazil striker Marta Vieira da Silva gave a rallying speech to young and aspiring female soccer players after her side was knocked out of the competition by tournament hosts France.

"Women's football depends on you to survive. Think about it, value it more. We're asking for support, you have to cry at the beginning and smile at the end. It's about wanting more, it's about training more, it's about looking after yourself more, it's about being ready to play 90 minutes and then 30 minutes more. So that's why I am asking the girls. There's not going to be a Formiga forever, there's not going to be a Marta forever, there's not going to be a Cristiane."

EUROPEAN CHAMPIONSHIPS

Also known as the Euros, this international tournament began in 1960 and features national teams from all over Europe. The Euros, just like the World Cup, are played every four years. They can be hosted by a single country or by lots at once, with the 2020 Euros being played all across Europe. The most successful teams in the Euros have been Spain and Germany, each winning it three times. Spain won the tournament twice in a row with their brilliant tiki-taka technique and Barcelona-heavy teams of 2008 and 2012 (see p. 17).

AFRICAN CUP OF NATIONS

Shortened to "AFCON," the African Cup of Nations has been running since 1957, when only three national teams took part: Sudan, Egypt, and Ethiopia. Now 24 national teams compete in the tournament, which usually takes place every two years. There have been 16 winners at AFCON: Egypt, United Arab Republic, Ethiopia, Ghana, Congo-Kinshasha, Sudan, Congo, Zaire, Morocco, Nigeria, Cameroon, Algeria, Ivory Coast, South Africa, Tunisia, and Zambia.

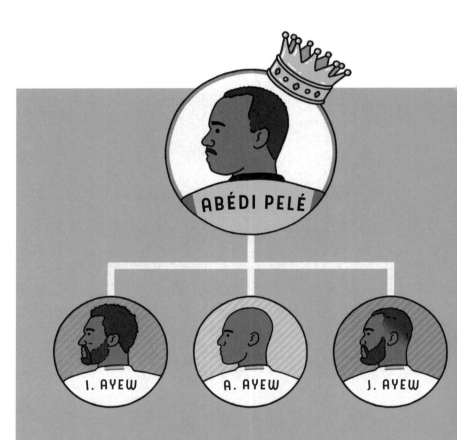

The Ghanaian player Abédi "Pelé" Ayew was crowned player of the tournament at the 1992 AFCON, hosted by Senegal. Abédi played for French team Olympique de Marseille and the following year would go on to win the European Cup with them, helping them to become the only French club to ever win the competition. Abédi has three sons—Ibrahim, André, and Jordan—who are all professional soccer players...and have all played for Ghana.

OLYMPIC GAMES

Since 1900, men's soccer has been a sport in the Olympic Games. Only amateur teams and under-23-year-old players, with the exception of three players, are allowed to play in the men's tournament. Women's soccer has been featured since 1996.

THE AFC ASIAN CUP

This cup is played by national teams from across Asia. This cup has been held every four years since 1956, although after the 2004 cup it was brought forward a year to stop it from clashing with the Summer Olympics and the Euros. Japan are the most successful team, with four tournament victories, with Saudi Arabia and Iraq in joint second, having won three each.

COPA AMÉRICA

The oldest men's international tournament in the world, the Copa América features national teams from South America and, since 1993, teams from Asia and North America, too. Uruguay won the first competition in 1916 and has gone on to become its most successful team, winning 15 in total.

❶ LIGUE 1

Location: France
Founded: 1930
Most Titles: Saint-Étienne (10)
Top Goalscorer: Delio Onnis—299
A big moment: Between 2002–08, Olympique Lyonnais won seven titles in a row.

❷ NWSL

Location: USA
Founded: 2012 (after Women's Professional Soccer in 2007 and Women's United Soccer Association in 2001)
Most Titles: FC Kansas City and Portland Thorns FC (2)
Top Goalscorer: Samantha Kerr—64
A big moment: In 2002, Michelle Akers, who started at University team UCF Knights, wins FIFA Female Player of the Century.

❸ LA LIGA

Location: Spain
Founded: 1929
Most Titles: Real Madrid (33)
Top Goalscorer: Lionel Messi—419, and counting
A big moment: In 2009, Barcelona became the first Spanish team to win the treble of La Liga, the Copa del Rey, and the Champions League.

❹ FAWSL

Location: England
Founded: 2010 (formerly FA Women's National League, founded in 1992)
Most Titles: Arsenal (3)
Top Goalscorer: Nikita Parris—37
A big moment: Vivianne Miedema scored 22 goals for Arsenal during the 2018–19 season, seven more than any previous top

❺ SERIE A

Location: Italy
Founded: 1898
Most Titles: Juventus (35)
Top Goalscorer: Silvio Piola—274
A big moment: In 1987, Diego Maradona arrived in Naples and led them to their first ever league title.

❻ DIVISION 1 FÉMININE

Location: France
Founded: 1974
Most Titles: Olympique Lyonnais (17)
Top Goalscorer: Ada Hegerberg—130
A big moment: Since 2007, Olympique Lyonnais have won the league every single year.

❼ J-LEAGUE

Location: Japan
Founded: 1992
Most Titles: Kashima Antlers (8)
Top Goalscorer: Yoshito Ōkubo—179
A big moment: Dutch striker Henny Meijer scored the league's first ever goal for Tokyo Verdy.

❽ CHINESE SUPER LEAGUE

Location: China
Founded: 2004
Most Titles: Guangzhou Evergrande Taobao (7)
Top Goalscorer: Wu Lei—102, and counting
A big moment: The World Cup-winning Italian coach Marcello Lippi led Guangzhou Evergrande Taobao to three titles in a row between 2012 and 2014.

❾ MLS

Location: USA and Canada
Founded: 1993
Most Titles: LA Galaxy (5)
Top Goalscorer: Chris Wondolowski—149, and counting
A big moment: In 2020, Inter Miami—a team owned by David Beckham—will enter the league pyramid.

❿ THE PREMIER LEAGUE

Location: England and Wales
Founded: 1992 (although the top flight of English soccer has been going since 1888)
Most Titles: Manchester United (20)
Top Goalscorer of all time: Jimmy Greaves—357
Top Goalscorer since Premier League formation: Alan Shearer—260 goals
A big moment: The relegation favorites, Leicester City won the title in 2016.

⓫ A-LEAGUE

Location: Australia
Founded: 2004 (previously National Soccer League from 1974)
Most Titles: Melbourne Victory and Perth Glory (4)
Top Goalscorer: Besart Berisha—116
A big moment: In 2018, Central Coast Mariners offered 100m world-record holder Usain Bolt a professional contract.

AMAZING STADIUMS

There is hardly anything that feels as exciting as approaching a stadium on game day. The smells, and the colors, and the sounds, and the prospect of watching your team lose 4–0: unbeatable. Stadiums are big, imposing places where dreams can be made or broken. Some of them stand out more than others. Here you will discover some of the most iconic soccer stadiums the world has to offer.

CAMP NOU

Barcelona's Camp Nou has the largest capacity of any soccer stadium in Europe. It can hold 99,354 spectators.

The seats one of the stands spell out the phrase "MORE THAN A CLUB" in Catalan, which is the club motto. Camp Nou has hosted many famous games, but not all of them have involved the Barcelona team. Camp Nou hosted the final five games of the 1982 World Cup and the Olympic soccer final in 1992, as well as the European Cup/Champions League final in 1989 and 1999.

In the 1989 European Cup final, Milan coach Arrigo Sacchi played some of the best Italian players of the time: Galli, Tassotti, Costacurta, Baresi, Maldini, Donadoni, Ancelotti, and Colombo alongisde Dutch players Rijkaard, Gullit, and Van Basten.

The 1999 Champions League final was Manchester United's famous comeback against Bayern Munich. United were 1–0 down until Teddy Sherringham and Ole Gunnar Solskjaer scored to win the cup and complete United's treble of 1999, made up of the Premier League, FA Cup, and Champions League titles.

LA BOMBONERA

La Bombonera is the home of Boca Juniors in Argentina. In Spanish, La Bombonera means "the chocolate box." The stadium is called this because the shape of the building reminded the club president of a box of chocolates.

La Bombonera was built in 1940 and holds 49,000 people. The stadium has amazing acoustics (the way in which sound projects and travels around a building). The supporters are called *la doce*, which means "the twelfth man," because they are so supportive, they are as helpful as having a twelfth player.

Don't be fooled by the sweet name, the Chocolate Box is renowned as one of the most intimidating soccer stadiums to play at in the world.

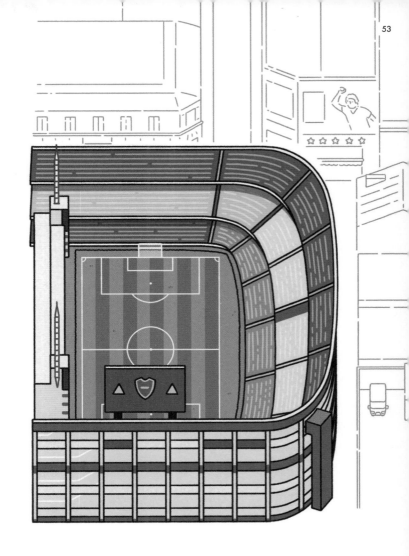

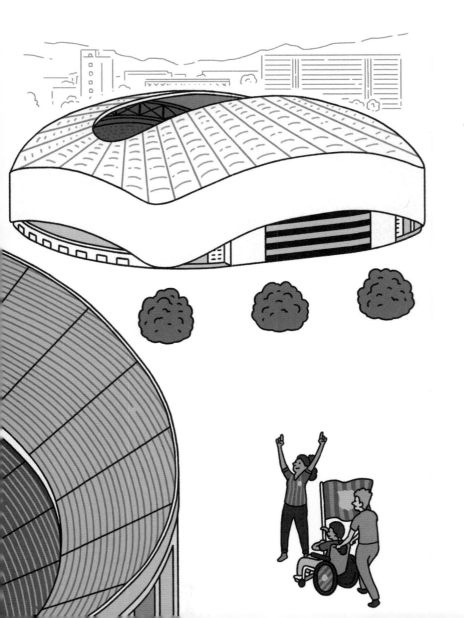

STADE VÉLODROME

This stadium has a very distinctive domed roof and is home to the Olympique de Marseille team in France. The Vélodrome can hold 67,394 people, and if all the rows of seats were put side by side, they would measure over 32 miles.

The Vélodrome hosted two games at the 1938 World Cup, six games at Euro 2016, and seven at the 1998 World Cup, including the quarter final between the Netherlands and Argentina, in which Dennis Bergkamp scored one of his greatest goals ever.

In the last five minutes of the Netherlands – Argentina game, the score was 1–1. With two minutes to go, Dutch player Frank de Boer launched the ball to Dennis Bergkamp, who kicked it between two Argentinian defenders, smashing it into the top corner of the goal and winning the game for the Netherlands.

WEMBLEY

Wembley Stadium is one of the most famous soccer stadiums in the world. Since its reopening in 2007, it can hold 90,000 fans and is home to England's national soccer team.

Wembley was briefly the home of Tottenham Hotspur, while their new stadium at White Hart Lane was under construction between 2017 and 2019.

Wembley Stadium hosts the FA Cup final every year. It has also hosted seven Champions League finals. For England the most important game played here was the 1966 World Cup final. England beat West Germany 4–2. Geoff Hurst scored a hat trick and Bobby Moore lifted the iconic Jules Rimet trophy.

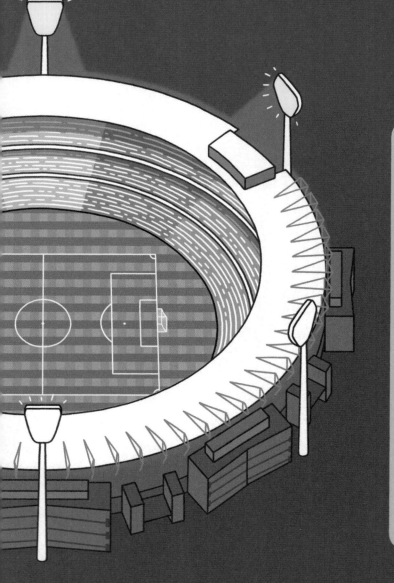

MELBOURNE CRICKET GROUND

The Melbourne Cricket Ground is the tenth-largest stadium in the world. Built all the way back in 1853 and with a capacity of 100,024, it's a big, big old stadium and the largest in the Southern Hemisphere.

It hosts Aussie Rules Football in the winter and cricket in the summer. The first soccer game hosted there was between Victoria and Tasmania in 1912, and it hosted the Olympic Games in 1956.

Lots of teams play at the MCG when they tour during the off-season. When Manchester City took on Real Madrid in the International Champions Cup in 2014, 99,382 fans went to watch.

WESTFALENSTADION

Westfalenstadion is home to Borussia Dortmund. The stadium is also known as Signal Iduna Park and can hold 81,365 fans.

The Südtribüne is the name for the standing area of the stadium. It is the biggest standing area in any European stadium and can hold 24,454 people. It is nicknamed the Yellow Wall because when the fans hold their yellow scarves and flags it looks like a big wall of yellow.

One of the stands at Tottenham Hotspur's new White Hart Lane stadium is modeled on Westfalenstadion's *Südtribüne*.

In 2006, Germany played Italy at Westfalenstadion in the World Cup semifinals. The score was 0–0 after 90 minutes, and it went to extra time. It looked as though the game would go to penalties, but Fabio Grosso and Alessandro Del Piero scored in the 119th and 120th minutes to put Italy into the World Cup final and make the German fans cry.

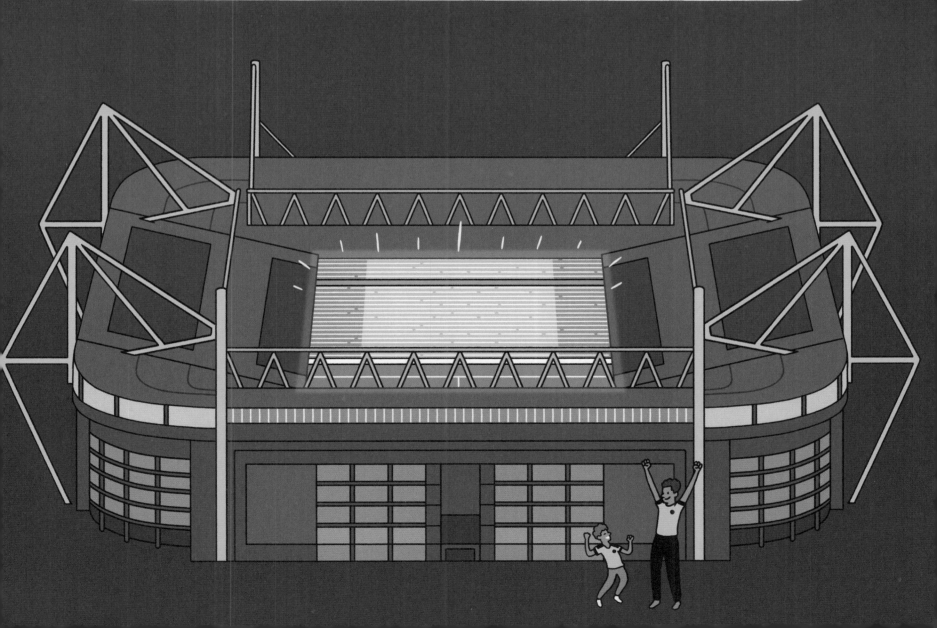

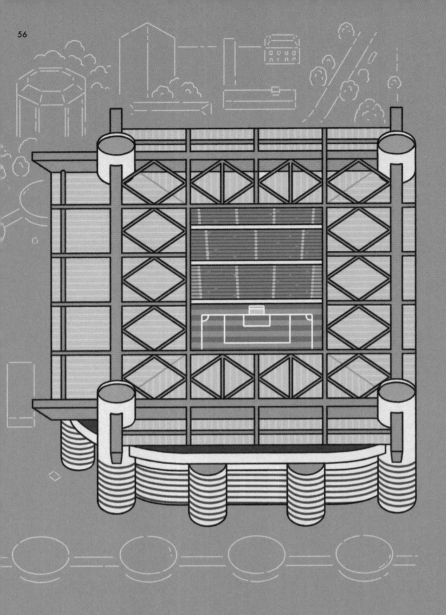

SAN SIRO

Also known as the Giuseppe Meazza Stadium, San Siro is home to both A.C. Milan and Internazionale, nicknamed "Inter." It holds 80,018 spectators and is one of the oldest and most famous grounds.

San Siro hosted six of the 1990 World Cup games, as well as Champions League finals in 1965, 1970, 2001, and 2016. Three of the games at the 1934 World Cup were also played at San Siro.

In 2003, A.C. Milan had to play Inter in the Champions League semifinals, which are played over two games. If the score is tied at the end of those games, whichever team scored the most goals away from home go through. However, A.C. Milan and Inter were both playing at home in both legs! The first ended 0–0, and the second ended 1–1. You would think that this result meant a draw. But, before the games took place, it had been decided that the first leg would count as A.C. Milan's home game, and the second leg would count as Inter's home game. This meant that A.C. Milan went through on away goals, despite both teams playing at home for both legs. How confusing!

SOCCER CITY

South Africa held the continent's first ever World Cup in 2010, a tournament that screamed with the sound of the vuvuzela, a plastic horn that everyone in the crowd seemed to have.

The final was held here, in Johannesburg, in the brilliantly named Soccer City. Imagine a city just for soccer! It's also known as the First National Bank Stadium, which isn't as fun, or the Calabash, which is the name of a traditional African pot that it resembles. During the league, it's the home for Kaizer Chiefs FC who play in the South African Premier Soccer League.

The stadium was where Nelson Mandela, an incredibly important man who fought for equality between races in South Africa, gave a speech when he was released from jail. It's an important place, and the World Cup final saw over 84,000 people watch Iker Casillas lift the cup.

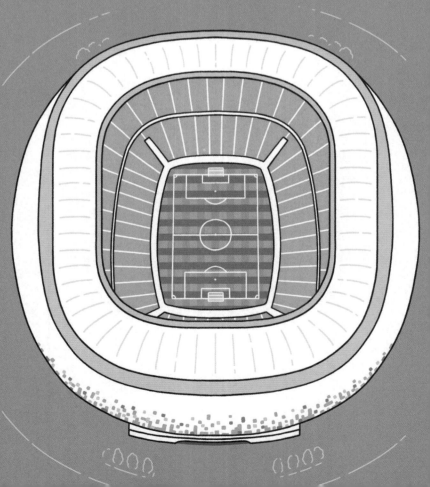

THE ROSE BOWL

In the summer of 1994, the World Cup was held in the United States of America for the first time. The final of the tournament, Brazil v. Italy, was played at the Rose Bowl, a huge roofless stadium in Pasadena, a suburb of Los Angeles, in California. The stadium holds 92,542 people and was completely packed for the final.

The game itself, played after four weeks of games in the heat, was a slow-burner and was 0–0 after both 90 minutes and extra time: the first and last World Cup final to have no goals throughout. It went to penalties, which Brazil won 3–2, with Roberto Baggio—nicknamed *Il Divin Codino*, meaning the Divine Ponytail, because of his hair—missing the decisive penalty. Baggio was distraught, the Brazilians were ecstatic, and the Rose Bowl had seen one of the strangest World Cup finals of all time.

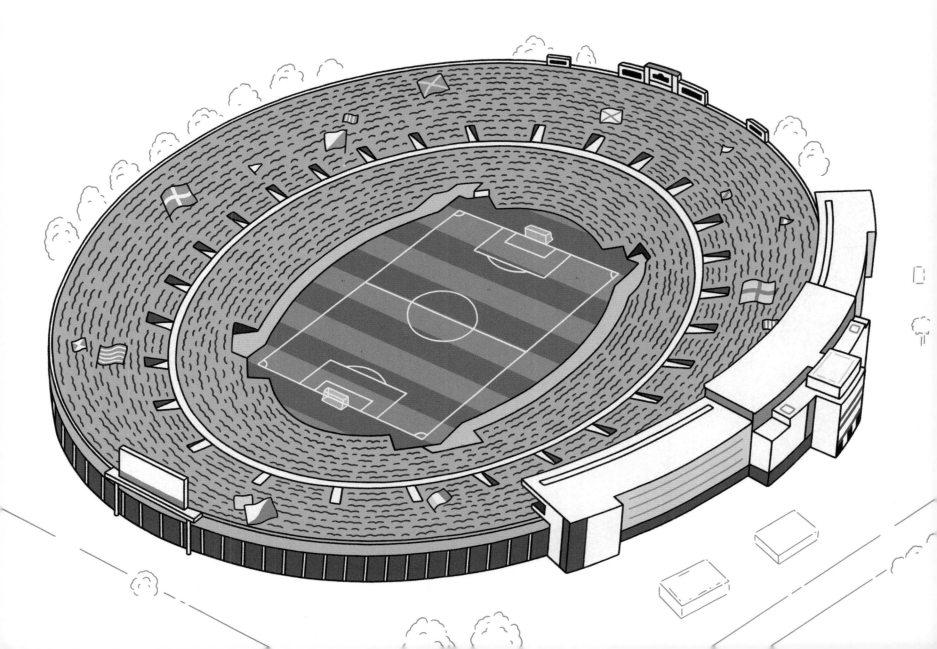

UNIFORMS HALL OF FAME

Is there any better feeling than putting on your favorite soccer uniform? On a practical level, soccer shirts are there to help players identify who is on their team so they can pass the ball to them. But to fans and to players, they mean much, much more. They're not just for wearing on the field, they're for wearing when you're with your friends, or having dinner, or practicing in the yard. Soccer uniforms are sometimes amazing, sometimes silly, and sometimes not-so-great...These are our pick of the bunch. What do you think?

PLYMOUTH ARGYLE (UK), 1965

The beautiful green and black horizontal stripes of this uniform contrast perfectly with the fresh white of the jersey. The big crest with the billowing sails of the *Mayflower* ship adds real drama right in the middle of the shirt.

USSR, 1966

The USSR's (now Russia) 1966 uniform was a plain red sweatshirt with "CCCP" written across the front. In Russia they use a different alphabet, and this spelled USSR. The design was simple but a classic.

MARSEILLE (FRANCE), HOME, 1971

This uniform has plain white shorts and a smart crew-neck collar featuring the colors of the French flag. The word "BUT," which means "GOAL" in French, is bravely smacked across the front of it in capital letters.

NETHERLANDS, HOME, 1972
SPECIFICALLY JOHAN CRUYFF'S

Puma and adidas were founded by rival brothers. Cruyff was sponsored by Puma, but the shirt was made by adidas. To stay loyal to Puma, Cruyff ripped the third stripe off the arm of his adidas shirt and managed to make it look cooler in the process.

NEW YORK COSMOS (USA), HOME, 1979

This uniform was designed by Ralph Lauren and has a striking logo. The large numbers are bold and stylish. It was worn by Carlos Alberto and Franz Beckenbauer, which helps add to its iconic status.

BOCA JUNIORS (ARGENTINA), HOME, 1981

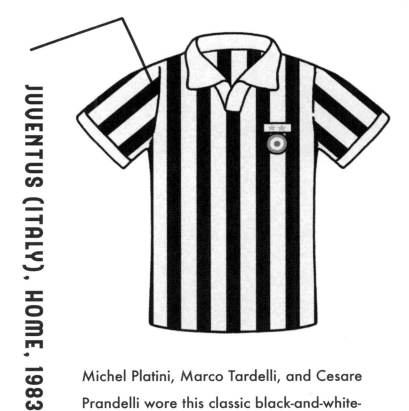

If you see a blue shirt with a big horizontal yellow stripe across the middle, it can only be one team: Boca Juniors. The shirt is classic, simple, and timeless.

LAZIO (ITALY), HOME, 1982

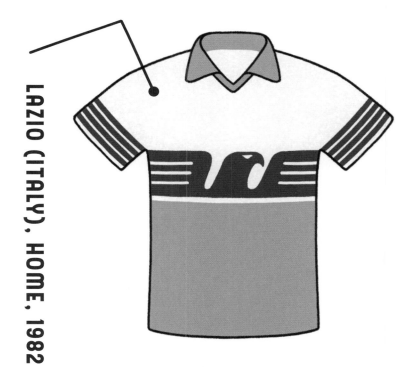

This shirt has an eagle with its wings spread, in the team colors, right over the front. Very nice, Lazio, *bravissimo*!

JUVENTUS (ITALY), HOME, 1983

Michel Platini, Marco Tardelli, and Cesare Prandelli wore this classic black-and-white-striped number with a massive white collar. They looked fantastic in it.

DENMARK, HOME, 1986

A harlequin-style shirt split into quarters, and two of those quarters have super-thin red and white stripes on them. The players who wore it became style itself.

HOLLAND, HOME, 1986

With adidas stripes down the sleeves, a cool pattern that makes it look like a reflector for your bike and traditional orange with chunky black numbering, this shirt belongs in the hall of fame.

MANCHESTER CITY (UK), AWAY, 1988

brother

A gorgeous shirt covered in burgundy and white stripes, with a traditional sky-blue collar and the sponsor "brother" emblazoned on the chest.

WEST GERMANY, HOME, 1988

This black-and-white shirt is such a classic that it was remade in 2018, and it looked just as good second time around.

GRÊMIO (BRAZIL), HOME, 1990

You just don't see thick black and sky-blue stripes separated by narrower white stripes enough on soccer uniforms these days.

ENGLAND, HOME, 1990

With Umbro tape around the sleeves and a crisp collar, this shirt is so nice you could almost get away with wearing it to a wedding.

SAMPDORIA (ITALY), HOME, 1991

This shirt's colors, design, and badge come together in perfect harmony to make a very stylish piece.

MARSEILLE (FRANCE), HOME, 1992

The three light blue stripes coming over the shoulder are like a pat on the back from a giant three-toed bear. It's no wonder they won the Champions League.

AUSTRALIA, HOME, 1993

This is a legendary piece of sports clothing. The media called it "the pizza vomit shirt" and, well, they were probably right. The Aussies wore it for their unsuccessful qualifying campaign for the 1994 World Cup, and it's possible that nobody has worn it since.

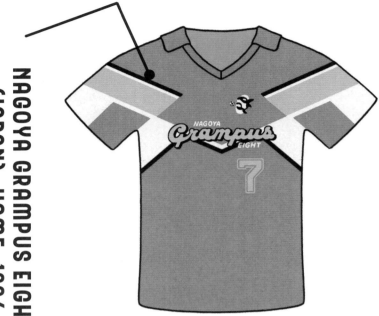

NAGOYA GRAMPUS EIGHT (JAPAN), HOME, 1994

Arsène Wenger's team wore these red jerseys with diagonal yellow and white stripes in 1994. They each had their own name plastered over the chest, where a sponsor's name would usually be.

USA, AWAY, 1994

The stars stretched over the shirt make it look like the US flag billowing in the wind. It shall remain hoisted at full mast in this book for evermore.

ESTONIA, GOALKEEPER, HOME, 1997

Like your grandma's favorite curtains that she flat out refuses to get rid of, but somehow good.

MEXICO, HOME, 1998

This design combines Aztec patterns and the giant face of the Aztec god of death in various shades of green. A masterpiece.

FRANCE, AWAY, 2013

This is very similar to the classic '70s Marseille uniform but with a polo-shirt-style collar and a classy duck-egg-blue color.

MADUREIRA SPORTING CLUB (CUBA), GOALKEEPER, HOME, 2013

The whole shirt was a Cuban flag with a big picture of Cuban leader Che Guevara on it. You either love this one or you hate it.

NIGERIA, HOME, 2018

This shirt features 1990s-style zigzag stripes. It is green and white on the body and black and white on the sleeves. It was easily the best uniform at World Cup 2018.

JAPAN WOMEN'S, HOME, 2019

The 2019 World Cup was the first where women had uniforms designed specifically for... women. It is ridiculous that it took so long for this to happen. There were some great shirts in this World Cup, but this was probably the best.

HOW TO...

Now you know the history of the game, let's learn how to play
it like a pro. You don't have to be the best player in the world to
enjoy it—soccer is about running around on a piece of grass with
your friends, but it's also fun to get better at it. And Coach Chris
is going to help you get up to scratch.

Hey, I'm Coach Chris. The players I'm going to introduce you to are the very best in the world in their particular area. I'm nowhere near as good as them, but what I do know is how they did it, and I'm here to tell you.

Together, we will look at the most amazing skills and then I will show you, step by step, how players made them look so easy. Then you can go and practice them for yourself.

Let's go.

HOW TO TAKE THE PERFECT SHOT
LIKE JI SO-YUN

Being able to finish, or take a good shot, is crucial in soccer. It's how you're going to score most of your goals. And Ji So-yun is very good at scoring goals. When she is bearing down on a goal, she is usually going at full speed, causing havoc in the opposition defense, limbs moving all over the place to distract the defenders. But in her head, all is calm.

If you see an opportunity to shoot, start thinking about the ball and the ball only. It's just you and the ball. The goal will stay exactly where it is.

1. Glance up to see where the goalie is. You're going to have to either hit the ball very hard and accurately, or trick them somehow.

2. Fix your eyes on the ball and think about how you're going to hit it. With curl? With power? With absolute accuracy?

CURL   ACCURACY   POWER   CURL

GOAL!

4. Don't stop your foot when you get to the ball. Follow through with your laces, your leg, and your whole body.

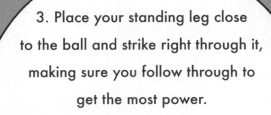

3. Place your standing leg close to the ball and strike right through it, making sure you follow through to get the most power.

All good strikers know exactly where the goal is, no matter where they are on the field. The goal doesn't move, so always keep that in mind.

JI SO-YUN

Born in 1991, Ji So-yun grew up in Seoul in South Korea. She started her career playing at INAC Kobe Leonessa. She moved to Chelsea in 2013, and is now considered one of the best players in the world. Ji is the youngest ever goal scorer for South Korea. She was only 15 years and 282 days old when she scored her first international goal, and is now South Korea's all-time top scorer. Ji also scored the only goal in the first FA Women's Cup Final to be held at Wembley Stadium in 2015.

Bonus tip: Try asking your goalkeeper friends what type of shots they find most difficult to save, then practice those shots until you can do them with your eyes closed.

HOW TO MAKE THE PERFECT SLIDE TACKLE
LIKE ALESSANDRO NESTA

To do a great slide tackle, you have to be certain of what is going to happen in two or three seconds' time, otherwise you'll commit a foul or hurt your opponent. Try and figure out where the players around you are heading and where they will be. Alessandro Nesta was good at slide tackling because he watched and played so much soccer that he always knew what his opponent was going to do. And, by learning so much from watching, he could commit himself to a heroic, beautiful sliding tackle.

1. Analyze where the ball is now and how fast the opposition player who has the ball is running. Which way are they likely to run and how quickly? When are you most likely going to be able to steal the ball? Anticipation is key.

2. Start your maneuver. Run at the right pace for where you expect the ball to be when you're going to make your tackle. Head toward that spot and get ready to make your slide.

LONGEST SLIDE TACKLE EVER

Born in 1974 in Plaistow, East London, Sol Campbell was the youngest of 12 children. He was an amazing soccer player as a child and trained at England's prestigious schoolboy training camp Lilleshall. Sol won lots of trophies, mostly for Arsenal. A slide tackle he made in the 24th minute of a game while playing for England against Croatia is considered the longest slide tackle ever. Many people say he's still sliding now, but they are exaggerating.

ALESSANDRO NESTA

Nesta is one of the greatest defenders of all time, having won the Serie A award for Defender of the Year four times. When Nesta was playing, Serie A was known for its impeccable defenders, so to be named the best in Italy four times is quite an honor. Nesta also won Serie A three times, the Champions League twice with A.C. Milan, and the World Cup with Italy in 2006.

5. Get up, move away from the opposition, and hold on to possession.

3. Once you're close, start to think about putting all of your weight toward the ground so that you can slide smoothly toward the ball.

4. Slide on your thigh, with your other leg stretched toward the ball. Move all of your weight toward that foot and slide straight through the ball, aiming to hook it toward your body to keep possession.

One of the secrets to Nesta's success was that he put the ball first. When he tackled his opponent, he always made sure the ball stuck with him or moved away from danger. The perfect slide tackle should be clean, safe, and perfectly timed. So get out your crystal ball and your tea leaves and start predicting the future like Alessandro Nesta.

HOW TO TAKE THE PERFECT SET PIECE
LIKE DAVID BECKHAM

David Beckham was the king of curve. He had all the makings of a superstar with his boy band looks and immaculate passing, crossing, and shooting techniques. Beckham was a very talented young player, but he spent long hours training on his own in the local park in order to perfect his signature moves. He was notorious for putting curve on the ball, which made his set pieces difficult to defend against. His free kicks and corners would curve and swerve so impressively they seemed to defy physics.

1. Place the ball in a tuft of grass that allows your foot to connect cleanly. Make sure the ball doesn't sit too high on the long grass or the ball will loop too high when kicked. Also, don't squash the ball too deep into the tuft or it will be hard to get enough lift.

2. Look at where your teammates are, or if you're practicing on your own, think about where they would be. You want to curve the ball so it reaches them at just the right moment.

3. Now focus on the ball. Think about which part of it you want to hit with your foot. Striking it to the left or right of the middle means it will spin in the air and curl, making it difficult for defenders to follow it. You want a nice big arc.

Sounds difficult, but once you start to hit it sweetly, you won't want to stop. You'll be curving the ball all day. You can practice by finding a bucket, setting it up at different heights, and trying to kick the ball into the bucket without the ball bouncing.

5. Make sure you follow through with your foot after you connect with the ball. You want to get enough pace on the ball for it to confuse defenders and reach your teammate, who can tap it into the net.

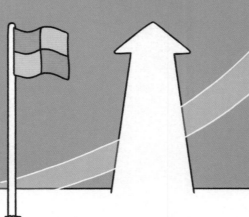

4. Start your run toward the ball and place your non-kicking foot close to it, then move your foot through the ball, connecting with the part that is between the top of your foot and the side. Keep practicing until you start to perfect this skill.

DAVID BECKHAM

Becks is one of the most famous soccer players of the past 30 years, and for good reason. He was the first English player to win the top league in four different countries: England (Manchester United), Spain (Real Madrid), Italy (A.C. Milan), and the USA (LA Galaxy).

He was a set piece specialist, and once scored from the halfway line on the opening day of the Premier League season in 1996.

In 1998 he almost ruined his reputation. He was fouled when playing against Argentina in a World Cup game. He was so frustrated that he kicked Diego Simeone (later the famous coach of Atlético Madrid), who stumbled to the ground. Beckham was sent off for his behavior. England lost 4–3 on penalties and was knocked out of the World Cup.

The newspapers said nasty things about young David, but he reacted in the right way. Instead of getting angry or hiding from his mistakes, he practiced and trained as hard as he could, and made himself into one of the best midfielders in the world, eventually being signed by Real Madrid and regaining the respect of soccer fans across the world.

HOW TO PLAY THE PERFECT LONG BALL
LIKE XABI ALONSO

Liverpool fans used to sing, "He is the midfield maestro, and his passes are so delightful, everybody wants to know, Al-on-so, Al-on-so, Al-on-so," and he is the long-ball hero. The long ball or long pass is very important because it means you can reach a teammate of yours on the other side of the field while taking the opposition players out of the game.

1. The first thing you should do whenever you get the ball is look up from the ball and around yourself. When you're planning to play a long ball, take a look at who has space around them for you to send it to.

2. Decide who you are passing to. Move the ball to your stronger foot and think about whether you want the ball to go straight to your teammate's feet or a little farther ahead of them so they can run onto it.

XABI ALONSO

Born in 1981, Xabi Alonso was a very clever central midfielder who played for Real Sociedad, Liverpool, Real Madrid, and Bayern Munich. He has won the World Cup, the European Championships, the Champions League, the FA Cup, La Liga, the Copa del Rey (Spanish Cup), the Bundesliga, and the DFB-Pokal (German Cup). He once scored from his own half for Liverpool against Newcastle United...a long ball straight into the goal. It was beautiful and unbelievable.

4. Strike through the ball with the laces on your shoe and start to move straightaway. Don't spend too long soaking up the glory from your amazing long ball. Your next job is to be in space to help your teammate out.

3. Who have you got to get it past, and how? Think about the height and weight of your kick. Do you want to hit it as hard as possible to get it over the opposition, or loop it up into the air slightly so that your teammate can take out one of the opposing players when they receive it?

When played well, the long ball can defeat a high press and be an effective counter-attacking technique. It can take multiple opponents out of the game in a short amount of time. They look great and kicking a ball far feels great.

HOW TO TAKE PENALTIES
LIKE MATT LE TISSIER

Penalties don't have an awful lot to do with technique. If you can kick a ball, you can take a penalty. The thing about penalties is that they are all in your head. They're all about mastering your nerves, making decisions, and having confidence in yourself when under pressure.

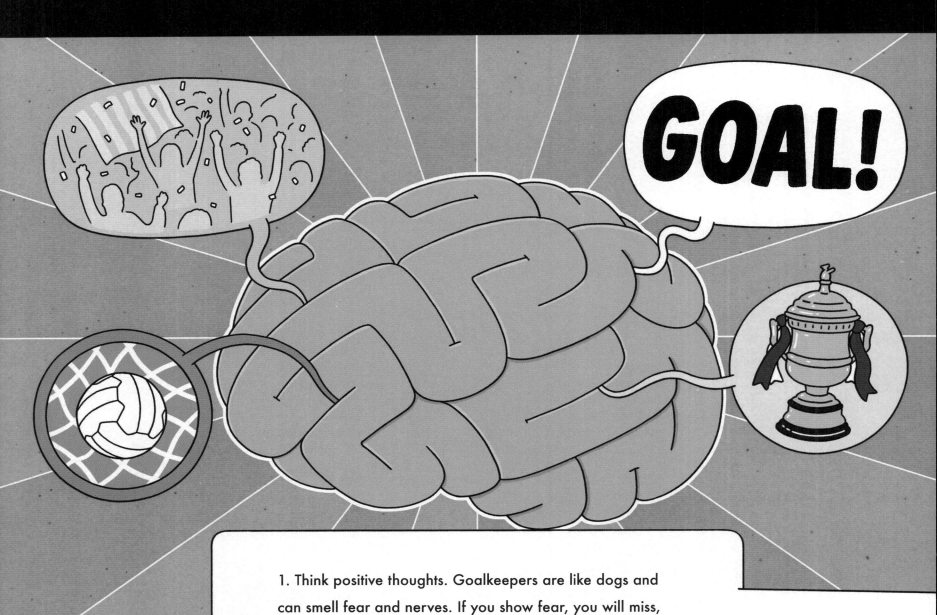

1. Think positive thoughts. Goalkeepers are like dogs and can smell fear and nerves. If you show fear, you will miss, so thinking positively is the most important thing.

3. Be adaptable. As you are about to kick, see if the goalie commits early to one side or the other. If you react quickly, you can roll the ball into the opposite corner to score an easy goal.

2. Pick a part of the goal to aim

MATT LE TISSIER

Matt Le Tissier was Southampton's star player of the 1990s. He regularly scored effortless wonder goals. He took 49 penalties in his career and only missed one of them.

That's a phenomenal record and even better than Lionel Messi and Cristiano Ronaldo. He was a bold decision maker, and this helped him put the ball in the back of the net time after time.

Bonus tip: Practice a lot and always put yourself forward to take a penalty in a game. It's a totally different feeling taking penalties in front of a crowd rather than in your backyard.

HOW TO DO NUTMEGS
LIKE LUIS SUÁREZ

To nutmeg somebody means to play the ball between their legs in order to get past them. Some people think that this term comes from cockney rhyming slang, in which legs are called nutmegs. The ball goes through your legs, or through your nutmegs. It's something that makes you feel a bit confused and then embarrassed if it happens to you, but if you do it, you feel pretty smart, and it is really useful. There are a few different ways of doing it.

1. Practice your reactions. Occasionally you will notice your opponent stood still, facing you, legs apart. If you're fast enough, you can knock the ball between their legs and run past them, watching as they try to figure out what just happened and which way they should turn.

3. Don't kick the ball too far through the opponent's legs. Remember that unless you are playing a pass through their legs, you will have to run around them and meet the ball at the other side.

2. Create a chance to nutmeg an opponent by feigning to run in a certain direction, and as the opponent moves to chase you, knock the ball between their now-open legs. Then sprint away, leaving the defender considering whether or not to just get their legs sewn together and hop instead of walking for the rest of their life.

LUIS SUÁREZ

Luis Suárez is really good at making a fool of himself, but he's much better at making fools out of opposition players. He has been banned for biting opponent players on three occasions in his career, and once stopped a goal from going in with his hand when Uruguay was playing Ghana in the World Cup quarter finals. He was sent off, but Ghana missed the subsequent penalty and ended up losing the game. Suárez, however, is an unbelievably good striker and an expert at nutmegging defenders.

Bonus tip: Give them the eyes. You know, freak them out. Look in one direction as though you're traveling that way, then head in the opposite direction. They'll move one leg, then you can pop the ball through the space between their legs.

HOW TO HAVE THE PERFECT FIRST TOUCH
LIKE DENNIS BERGKAMP

Your first touch is the way in which you adapt your body to control the ball when you receive it. You need to receive it in a way that makes your next step on the field easy. You might cushion it with your thigh, trap it under the sole of your foot, or take it in your stride while you run. The players with the best first touch make it look like they were born with a soccer ball next to them. Like Maradona, who even at the age of 10 used to be paid to do kick-ups in the center circle at professional club Argentinos Juniors. Oh, Diego!

1. Look around you before, or as the pass is on its way to you. Know where every player is on the field, especially the players closest to you, and decide whether you are going to shoot, pass, or dribble once you've controlled the ball.

2. Now you know where the other players are and what you're going to do with the ball, do not take your eye off it until you have controlled it.

4. Don't focus on just trapping the ball. Trapping the ball dead is sometimes useful, but often it just slows you down and means you have to waste time taking another touch to get the ball to where you need it to be. The longer you take to control the ball, the longer the opposition has to organize themselves and defend your attack.

DENNIS BERGKAMP

Dennis Bergkamp was a Dutch forward for Ajax, Inter, and Arsenal. Have you ever played that game where you and a friend have to throw an egg to each other from farther and farther away, and you have to be really careful not to break the egg when you catch it? That's how Dennis Bergkamp treated a soccer ball. He did not panic or use force when the ball came to him; he welcomed the ball. He cared for the ball. He probably tucked a soccer ball into bed at night and told it bedtime stories and sang lullabies to it. Soccer balls were obviously grateful for this tender, loving care, and tended to do whatever Bergkamp wanted them to do, which had something to do with them ending up in the back of the net in the next five seconds.

3. Judge the flight of the ball. Take notice of how quickly the ball is moving, whether it is spinning and whether the ball is on the floor or coming down from a height. These things will affect how you cushion the ball. If the ball is arriving fast and hard, try using the inside of your foot, allowing your foot to move backward with the ball slightly to bring the ball to a stop. If you just hold your foot in a fixed position, the ball will bounce off you and you will lose it.

LIKE XAVI

A "through ball" is a pass that is played forward, ahead of your teammate, so that they can run onto the ball. A through ball is usually played through a defensive line and is a great way to penetrate a stubborn defense, especially if the opposition is holding a high defensive line.

XAVI

Xavi Hernández was probably the best central midfielder of the 2000s and early 2010s. Xavi and Andrés Iniesta ran Barcelona and Spain's midfield in their most successful eras. It seemed as though they could read each other's minds, and they made lots of short passes while moving around the field quickly. Xavi's spatial awareness and ability to keep the opposition players at a distance was miraculous. Xavi achieved this by constantly picturing the game three or four seconds in the future.

1. Try to predict where the opposition defenders are going to move to next, where your teammates are going to run to, and where space is going to appear.

2. Pass the ball. Control the pace and weight of the kick so that your teammate can control, pass, or shoot with minimal effort. It is useful to kick the ball at the bottom or side to make it spin in the air and curve away from a defender and toward your teammate.

3. Make sure there is space behind the defense for your teammate to run into.

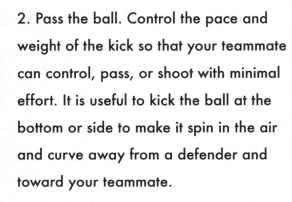

HOW TO BEAT THE OFFSIDE TRAP
LIKE FERNANDO TORRES

An offside trap is a defensive strategy in which the defenders form a straight line across the field and attempt to move forward at the same time in order to catch attackers offside when the ball is played to them. It's an effective tactic but a risky one and can leave a team vulnerable if a striker is an expert in beating the offside trap, like Fernando Torres.

1. Be fast.

2. Communicate with your teammates. Tell them when you want the ball to be played. Show them with your arms and with your voice. Discuss what sort of passes you like to receive before the game.

3. Time your run to perfection. The best way to do this is to position yourself a few yards back from the defensive line. Just as your teammate is about to pass to you, start sprinting at the defensive line, so that you are at full speed at the moment when they start running. This will allow you to reach the ball before the defenders without being caught offside.

FERNANDO TORRES

Beating the offside trap was Torres's special skill. He did this especially well in the 2012 Champions League semifinal for Chelsea against Barcelona. You cannot be offside if you are in your own half. When Barcelona pushed up to try and score a late goal, Torres waited near the halfway line in his own half, and when the ball was cleared toward him, he was able to sprint toward the goal without having to pass any defenders. The goal put Chelsea into the final, prompting commentator Gary Neville to make one of the strangest happy noises ever made by a human being, live on television.

HOW TO DO THE PERFECT ATTACKING HEADER
LIKE DIDIER DROGBA

An attacking header is a way of scoring a goal with your head. Your noggin. Your bean. More specifically your forehead. You use your forehead because it's the strongest part of your skull. Sometimes, you might want to use an attacking header as a pass to one of your teammates, but mostly you use this move when trying to score a goal.

1. Use the pace of the ball. A good cross needs plenty of speed and you must redirect the energy that the ball already has behind it.

2. Aim. Go for the corners of the goal and try to head the ball in the opposite direction than that of the keeper's movement.

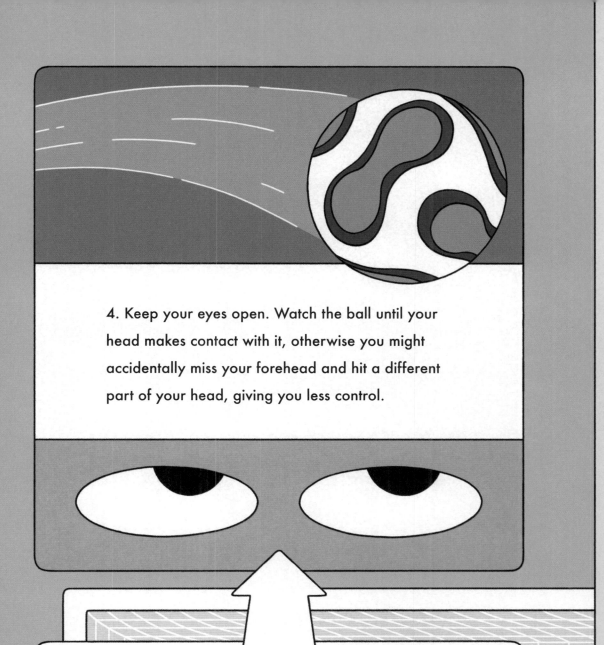

4. Keep your eyes open. Watch the ball until your head makes contact with it, otherwise you might accidentally miss your forehead and hit a different part of your head, giving you less control.

3. Head the ball downward with your forehead. Drogba would often attempt to head the ball downward, toward the goal and into the ground. It is more difficult to judge the flight of the ball if it is headed downward. It also means the keeper has to quickly get down to the ground in time to save it.

DIDIER DROGBA

Didier Drogba was born in Abidjan in the Ivory Coast, but as a child he moved away to live with his uncle on the outskirts of Paris. In 679 games for Le Mans, Marseille, and Chelsea, he scored 297 goals, as well as 65 goals in 105 games for his national Ivory Coast team. He won the African Footballer of the Year in 2006 and 2009, and even had a hand in halting a civil war in his home country. Among all of this, Didier was fantastic at heading the ball.

Bonus tip: If you head the ball toward the side of the goal where a cross has been hit from, you're most likely to trick the keeper into going the wrong way.

HOW TO DO THE PERFECT DEFENSIVE HEADER
LIKE KALIDOU KOULIBALY

A defensive header is a way of stopping and clearing an opposition team's attack with your head. It's used most often if the opposition has played a long ball—a big, aerial kick from goalkeepers or defenders that is aimed toward the strikers—or a cross from the wings. To slow down the attack, or stop it completely if at all possible, you want to get as much distance and air on the ball as possible...and if the attack is looking super dangerous, just head the ball out for a throw-in or corner. Get rid of it!

1. Jump! You don't have to be tall. What you lack in height, you can make up for by jumping.

3. Practice your timing. If you jump too quickly or too late to meet the ball, the move will be doomed.

2. Be strong and don't allow attackers to muscle you off the ball. You must be able to stand your ground. You don't have to be big, but you have to be steadfast.

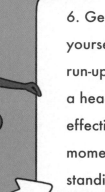

6. Get in position. Aim to give yourself space to have a little run-up for your jump. Performing a header after a run-up is most effective. It gives you more momentum than jumping from standing still.

5. Always use your forehead and make sure you attack the ball instead of letting the ball hit you. If you don't, it might hurt.

4. Get the ball to safety. If you can safely head the ball to a teammate, fantastic. If you can't, focus instead on distance and height, to give your team a chance to regroup and reorganize.

KALIDOU KOULIBALY

Born in France in 1991 to Senegalese parents, Kalidou Koulibaly moved from Metz in France, to Genk in Belgium, to Napoli in Italy, where his talents truly flourished. Under coach Maurizio Sarri, Kalidou became one of the greatest defenders in the world. His positioning, reading of the game, tackling, and heading are incredible. You'd do very well to get past Kalidou Koulibaly.

Bonus tip: Scream or shout your name, or your nickname, as loud as you can when attacking the ball. It makes you sound scary, and might distract the opposition player.

WEIRD AND WONDERFUL

The aim of the game is to get the ball into a goal and to stop your opponent from scoring. What could be more straightforward? But soccer is very strange. From the way we describe things that happen in the game (a fox in the box) to the way we celebrate a goal (by pretending to be a robot) or do our hair (shaving it all off except for a triangle at the front)...deep down, we all know that the reason we love soccer is because it is a strange old game.

THE HAIRCUTS

When you have to wear exactly the same uniforms as your teammates, hair is one of the few ways you can show the world your individuality. Here are some of the strangest and best haircuts in the game.

DAVID BECKHAM'S MOHAWK

Becks is famous for his trend-setting, varied hairstyles over the years, but the Mohawk is probably the most iconic. Soon after he debuted his new chop, kids all over the world started to request the "Beckham Mohawk."

TARIBO WEST'S GREEN BUNCHES

Taribo West was a hero of the 1996 Olympics and part of the famous Nigeria side, who won the tournament—the first African nation ever to do so. Taribo's signature look was to have no hair except for two green bunches tied tight on top of his head. It's a very bold look.

AJARA NCHOUT'S STYLE

Cameroonian forward Ajara Nchout has played all over the world, from Sweden to Russia to the States to Norway, scoring tons of goals along the way. All the while, she never fails to have amazing hair.

PAUL POGBA'S ARTISTRY

Paul Pogba's hair is art. He has had all sorts of shaved and dyed looks. Most famously he had leopard print and red-and-orange flames on the sides of his head.

CARLOS VALDERRAMA'S BLOND 'FRO

Valderrama was instantly recognizable on the field. The Colombian number 10 sported a giant, blond, Afro-style haircut topped off with a big, equally magnificent mustache. Carlos Valderrama: great at soccer, terrible at hide-and-seek.

CHRIS WADDLE'S MULLET

It may be strange to think that in the 1980s, the mullet was fashionable, but it was and Waddle had a magnificent one. Waddle worshipped the mullet. He was best friends with the mullet, and he couldn't let it go.

THE ENTIRE ROMANIA WORLD CUP SQUAD OF 1998

Romania had a team meeting just before the start of World Cup '98 in France. At this team meeting, the coach told his players that if they qualified for the knock-out rounds after two games, he would shave his head. The players told him that if he did that, then in return they would all dye their hair blond. It happened, and they all looked great.

RONALDO'S NOTHING BUT BANGS

This is probably the strangest thing that has ever been on a person's head, but if you're the best striker in the world, you can do whatever you like and people will still think it's cool. At the 2002 World Cup, Ronaldo de Lima turned up for Brazil with a completely shaved head, except for a triangle of hair at the front of his head that sort of looked like a third of a pizza.

MICHELLE AKERS

Look, Michelle Akers is one of the most fantastic soccer players ever to grace the sport. She won the FIFA Player of the Century award. Maybe her power came from her magnificent, voluminous hair.

DAVID SEAMAN'S PONYTAIL

David Seaman was Arsenal's legendary goalkeeper during the 1990s and 2000s. He was an outstanding goalkeeper but, unfortunately, he is remembered for two things. Firstly, for when Ronaldinho chipped him from about 35 yards away with a free kick in the England v. Brazil game at World Cup 2002. Secondly, for suddenly deciding that it would be a superb idea to grow a big shiny ponytail.

OLIVIER GIROUD

There is nothing funny about French forward Olivier Giroud's hair, and that's exactly why he is here. His hair is perfect. We don't know how he does it.

THE CELEBRATIONS

The history of the game, the evolution of the ball, and the changes in formation are all very important things to know about. But the best moment is when someone scores a goal. It is the best feeling in the world, and people celebrate in some bizarre ways. Here are some that were famous for specific players, and some that people all over the world do every day.

THE ONE HAND RAISED

This is a classic and was most famously employed by Alan Shearer, who was a brilliant striker. This celebration is simple, effective, and satisfying. It's a salute to the fans to let them know you love them.

THE KNEE SLIDE

Imagine that you're playing for your childhood club in your home debut. The fans are cheering you on. There are scarves with the team colors on everywhere. You pick up the ball just outside the box and curl in a goal. What does your brain tell you? "Knee slide. Do a big knee slide right over to the corner flag. That will be absolutely great!" So you do.

ROCKING THE BABY

This is quite a rare celebration that tends to be used by players who have just had a baby. Rocking the Baby was first used by Brazilian forward Bebeto, following the birth of his son during the 1994 World Cup in the USA. When you score a goal, how do you feel? Well, usually you feel very happy. Bebeto was obviously overjoyed to have a new baby boy, and so when he scored, he did what came naturally and thought of his son.

JUMPING INTO THE CROWD

This celebration does not come recommended, as you will almost certainly be shown a yellow card by the referee. However, in the past, people have felt the moment take them and you jump in and start hugging everyone around you while they chant your name. Sometimes you just have to go and hug the people who love you.

THE AIRPLANE

When you score a goal, sometimes it can feel as though you are flying and circling around the field looking down at all the unfortunate people who haven't scored a goal. Steve Bull did this particular move 306 times for Wolves.

THE STAND STILL WITH YOUR ARMS OUT

This is only to be used following absolutely jaw-dropping goals, otherwise you'll just look pretty silly. It says, "Look at me and feast your eyes upon the glorious player you see before you." Stand still and soak up the glory that is rightfully being showered upon you.

THE NO TIME TO WASTE

A move that is perfect for when time is running out. Imagine that your team is 3–1 down with five minutes to go. You score a goal, but you only have five minutes left to get the draw or the win. You want to get the ball back in play again as soon as possible, so you collect the ball and run it straight back to the center circle so the game can start again. There is no time for big celebrations here. After all, you're a team player and it's not all about you.

KISSING THE GRASS

You often hear people talking about the "hallowed turf" of a stadium, meaning that it is so special it is almost sacred. Kissing the grass is a show of respect to the place you love.

JUMPING ON THE COACH

Some players have bad relationships with their coaches and some players idolize them. If your coach has helped you with your technique and helped you through hard times, then the first thing you're going to want to do when you score is run over to them, jump on them and give them a big hug. Never forget that coaches need hugs too.

THE MILLA DANCE

Roger Milla from the Cameroon national team was the oldest ever World Cup goalscorer in 1990. He celebrated by dancing around the corner flag like a funky chicken.

THE RAPINOE POWER STATUE

Megan Rapinoe from the USA scores goals, and she scores them often. As an advocate for equality, Rapinoe said that she would not attend the White House to meet the president if the US won the World Cup because he is not an advocate for equality. President Trump responded and told her not to disrespect the country. The following game, Megan scored, stood still, raised her hands to the sky, grinned, and stood in an epic pose like a Greek statue. She stood in defiance of the president and stood for what she believed in. Many people recognized this as a wonderful power pose.

THE CANTONA LOOK-AROUND

Eric Cantona was great at soccer. On December 21, 1996, at a chilly Old Trafford, King Eric scored the most glorious of chips, leaving the goalkeeper to watch the ball dive-bomb into the very top corner of the goal, nestling into the net. Eric knew he was a special player, and he was too cool to celebrate an unbelievable goal. Goals are just what he does. Instead, he stood perfectly still and then looked around as if to say, "Yes, you did just see that. Believe your eyes."

BALOTELLI'S "WHY ALWAYS ME?"

There are lots of stories about the crazy things that Italian player Mario Balotelli has done during his career as a soccer player. Some of are them true; some of them false. Whatever happened during his time at Manchester City, all of the attention always seemed to end up on Super Mario. When he scored the first goal in a 6–1 win for City over Manchester United in 2011, he lifted up his shirt to reveal a message on his underlayer that read, "WHY ALWAYS ME?" Because you're unique, Mario, and we love you for it.

THE CROUCH ROBOT

England player Peter Crouch is 6 ft 7 in tall. Due to his height, spectators often said he looked awkward and uncoordinated. When Crouchy scored for England against Hungary in a pre–World Cup friendly in 2006, he decided to show the world that he was actually very coordinated indeed, thank you very much, and performed a robot dance in front of the whole world.

THE KLINSMANN

In 1990, Jürgen Klinsmann scored three goals for Germany at the World Cup. He had a very good tournament, but it is not his goals at the tournament that are remembered; it is his diving. In 1990s England, diving was considered a terrible form of cheating. So when Klinsmann arrived in England to play his first game for Tottenham Hotspur against Sheffield Wednesday in 1994, the crowd booed him. Klinsmann was a very talented striker and he scored a powerful header, after which he ran over to the side of the field and did a big dive onto the turf. Even the Wednesday fans laughed.

THE GOGGLES

Ellen White, the England international striker whose goals at the World Cup in 2019 saw England progress through the stages, has a trademark celebration: the Goggles. Ellen is from Aylesbury in England, and has played for Arsenal, Leeds, Birmingham, Notts County, Chelsea, and Manchester City, but she loves watching German soccer. After seeing Anthony Modeste put his hands around his eyes to make hand goggles, Ellen started doing it herself. In fact, she scores so many goals that she does the Goggles a lot.

THE BIGGEST, THE BEST, AND THE WEIRDEST

BIGGEST STADIUMS

DID YOU KNOW that the five biggest soccer stadiums (in terms of capacity) are in five different continents?

The **RUNGRADO 1ST OF MAY STADIUM** in Pyongyang, North Korea, holds 114,000 people—ASIA

The **MELBOURNE CRICKET GROUND** in Australia, home to the Socceroos, holds 100,024 people—OCEANIA

The **CAMP NOU** in Barcelona, Spain, holds 99,354 people—EUROPE

The **FNB STADIUM** in Johannesburg, South Africa, holds 94,736 people—AFRICA

The **ROSE BOWL STADIUM** in Pasadena, California, USA, holds 90,888 people—NORTH AMERICA

BIGGEST SCORE

On Halloween 2002, two Madagascan teams were playing each other in a play-off tournament. SO l'Emyrne were annoyed, as they thought that the referees had treated them unfairly in the previous games. They intentionally lost the game, going down 149–0 to their biggest rivals AS Adema.

BIGGEST CROWDS

199,854 spectators attended the 1950 World Cup final between Brazil and Uruguay at the Maracanã Stadium in Rio de Janeiro. At least 20,000 of the spectators didn't even have tickets.

DARREN BENT DOES LOVE TO BE BESIDE THE SEASIDE

In 2009, Sunderland were playing Liverpool in a Premier League game at the Stadium of Light. Five minutes into the game, Sunderland striker Darren Bent hit a low, pretty tame shot at the goal. Liverpool's goalie, Pepe Reina got down to gather the ball into his arms, but then something strange happened.

A Liverpool fan had brought a big red beach ball with him to the game. He threw the beach ball up in the air, and the wind blew it onto the field just at the moment that Bent took his shot. The soccer ball bounced off the beach ball and past Pepe Reina, who must've been wondering what on earth had just happened. The referee allowed the goal to stand and was later relegated to the Championship (the league below the Premier League) because of this. Sunderland went on to win the game 1–0, and the unfortunate Liverpool fan still feels guilty.

LARGEST PLAYER

The tallest soccer player in the world is Dulwich Hamlet's goalkeeper, Simon Bloch Jørgensen, who is 6 ft 10 in tall. Goalkeepers tend to be taller than outfield players, but if you're a goalkeeper and shorter than your friends, do not fear. Many people consider Reading's greatest ever goalkeeper to be Steve Death, who was 5 ft 7 in tall. There are two or three goalkeepers who were slightly shorter than Steve Death, but he also has probably the most rock 'n' roll name a soccer player has ever had. One more time: Steve Death.

SMALLEST PLAYER

The shortest male soccer players on record are Élton José Xavier Gomes and Daniel Alberto Villalva Barrios from Brazil and Argentina respectively. They are both just over 5 feet. It goes to show that height doesn't matter, as long as you practice your skills and put in lots of effort.

MOST HAT TRICKS

It is said that Pelé scored 92 career hat tricks. Some of these may have been in non-competitive games, but we'll give him the benefit of the doubt.

MOST SENT-OFF PLAYER

The player who has received the most red cards in their career is Colombian defender/midfielder Gerardo Alberto Bedoya Múnera, who was sent off 46 times. To put that into context, the player with the second most red cards is Cyril Rool with 27.

ODDEST RED CARDS

Lots of soccer players are superstitious. Many players have lucky cleats or shin pads. When Mukura Victory was playing Rayon Sport in the Rwandan Premier League in 2016, Victory's striker Moussa Camara was feeling particularly unlucky. He had missed several easy opportunities to score, and so he took matters into his own hands by placing a strange object on the goalposts and, apparently, casting a spell. The referee booked him for witchcraft, but Camara went on to score...mysterious!

Swedish player Adam Lindin Ljungkvist was once shown a second yellow card for farting during a reserve team game in Sweden. Ljungkvist states he had an upset stomach, but the referee disagreed. The ref said that Ljungkvist had purposefully provoked an opponent by farting toward them, and sent the defender off.

STIR-FRIED AIRPLANE

As we have already mentioned, fans use some clever, funny, and downright ridiculous words and phrases to describe things that happen in soccer (see p. 9). There is special soccer lingo in every language, and here are some of our favorite phrases, or idioms, from around the world.

炒飛機: STIR-FRIED AIRPLANE (CHINA)

A phrase used to describe a shot that has gone far wide or over. In English, we might say that the shot has been "spooned."

IMURI: VACUUM CLEANER (FINLAND)

In Finland, if you're a bad goalkeeper, then you'll be described as a vacuum cleaner: because you can't stop things from being sucked into the goal.

泥臭い: SMELLING OF MUD (JAPAN)

Not all goals are beautiful. In fact, loads aren't beautiful. They're scored by really forcing the ball over the line, something we might call a goalmouth scramble. In Japan, if it's a goal through determination rather than beauty, then it's described as smelling of mud.

HACER LA CAMA: TO MAKE THE BED (ARGENTINA)

Sometimes, a group of players will decide that their coach isn't doing the right thing, and essentially gang up on him. Really hammer him, stop trying, spread rumors. In Argentina, it's described as making his bed: "Go to sleep, Coach."

NA BANHEIRA: IN THE BATHTUB (BRAZIL)

If you are caught offside, this can be very annoying for your teammates, especially if they've worked hard to get to a position where they can play a pass to you. In Brazil, if this happened, they would say you are taking a bath because it is as though you are lazing around and not helping.

JEP NEST (TRINIDAD AND TOBAGO)

A jack spania, or a jep, is the Caribbean name for a wasp. Wasps like to nest in the top corners of things. So, if you shoot into the top corner of the net in Trinidad and Tobago, the ball has gone into the jep nest.

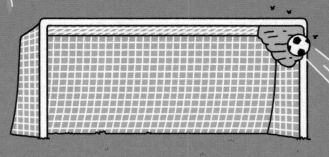

MINESTRA RISCALDATA: REHEATED SOUP (ITALY)

There are certain soccer coaches who go back to a club after they've already worked there before. In Italy, they'd describe this as reheated soup.

POTET: POTATO (NORWAY)

Potatoes are great. You can mash them, boil them, roast them, and turn them into fries. So, in Norway, if you're good at everything on the field and able to play in all positions, then you're a potato. A humble, versatile potato.

NABRAT NA SANE: TO TAKE SOMEONE ON A SLEIGH RIDE (CZECH REPUBLIC)

Sometimes slide tackles can go wrong, and you get completely wiped out by one with your legs in the air, your back bent, and your head somewhere else. In the Czech Republic, they say this is as though Santa has picked you up on his sleigh and off you go, all around to different houses.

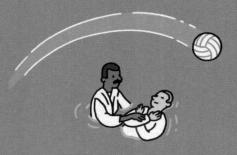

BAPTISER: TO BAPTISE (CAMEROON)

It's really annoying if a player scoops the ball over your head. It makes you feel silly. If it happens to you in Cameroon, they'll say you've been baptized.

MORE THAN THE GAME

You may think that soccer is just about what happens on the field: the magnificent goals, the soaring saves, and the big tackles that echo all around the stadium. But it's not. Much of what makes soccer, soccer, is the whole culture surrounding the game and the dedicated people who make the games possible. At a soccer game, the referee is as important as the striker. At a club, the nutritionist might make as much difference as the defensive coach. And the spirit of the crowd contributes as much to the atmosphere as the players.

RESPECTING THE REF

The referee, just like you, loves soccer. It is easy to forget that when you are playing or watching a game, but it is true. The decisions that they make allow us to play the game properly and fairly. It is essential to understand why and how they make the decisions they make and how they signal what their decision is.

IF THERE'S A GOAL...

The referee will blow their whistle and point to the center spot to show that the game now needs to be restarted by a kickoff.

IF SOMEONE IS OFFSIDE...

The assistant referee, who runs in line with the last defender, will raise their flag parallel with the ground. The referee will give a little toot on their whistle and wave their arm along the offside line. Keep playing until you hear that whistle, though: sometimes the ref will overrule the assistant refs.

IF THERE'S A DIRECT FREE KICK...

The referee will blow their whistle. Then they will point in the direction in which the team who has been awarded the free kick are kicking.

IF THERE'S AN INDIRECT FREE KICK...

The referee will blow their whistle and point straight toward the sky. An indirect free kick is a free kick from which you must pass the ball—you cannot shoot. They're awarded for offences such as a handball, a back pass that the goalkeeper picks up, or offensive language or dissent shown toward the referee.

IF THERE'S A THROW-IN...

The ref will blow their whistle and point in the kicking direction of the team who has won the throw-in.

IF THERE'S A GOAL KICK...

The ref will blow the whistle and point at the six-yard box.

IF THERE'S A CORNER...

The referee will point toward the corner and the assistant referee will point their flag toward the corner. If you score direct from a corner, it's called an olimpico.

IF THERE'S A HANDBALL...

If you purposely play the ball with your hand or arm, the other team will be awarded an indirect free kick or even a penalty if you're in your own penalty area.

Goalkeepers can obviously use their hands and arms, but only inside their own penalty area. If they handle the ball outside of the penalty area, an indirect free kick will be awarded to the opposition and the goalkeeper may be sent off!

IF THERE'S INJURY TIME...

The amount of injury time is calculated by the assistant referee, who writes it up on a board. If a game is stopped for ten minutes because of injuries during the game, ten minutes will be added on to the end of the 90-minute-game.

A RED CARD...

If you foul another player or commit a serious offense, then you will be given one of these and it means you need to leave the field immediately.

A YELLOW CARD...

This is a warning. If you do something bad, you'll get one of these. And if you get two, you will be sent off.

PIERLUIGI COLLINA

Pierluigi Collina was a really famous Italian referee. He was famous because of his shiny bald head and electric-blue eyes that made him absolutely terrifying. No player dared to argue with him, and he was the first referee to feature on the front cover of a *Pro Evolution Soccer* game.

THE OTHER JOBS

You don't have to be a soccer player to be a crucial member of the soccer club. Lots of people contribute to a game and in the run-up to a game. Here are a few of the important jobs that go on behind the scenes.

THE GROUNDSMAN

Soccer fields look beautiful, don't they? They need around-the-clock care to keep them level and make sure that the grass is hydrated, green, and luscious. If you like gardening and soccer, this could be the job for you.

THE KIT MAN

Sparkling clean uniforms and cleats don't appear magically. It is someone's job to wash, iron, and fold them. The kit man is a very important person—without them, players wouldn't look as good as they do.

THE NUTRITIONIST

This person tells the players what to eat for breakfast, lunch, dinner, and everything in between so that their bodies work like well-oiled machines when it comes to the big game.

THE PHYSICAL THERAPIST

These professionals treat injured players. You might see them rush onto the field to tend to a player who's just been involved in a nasty tackle or an awkward fall. You might see them struggling with a stretcher to take a player into the dressing rooms for treatment. They are highly skilled and very important.

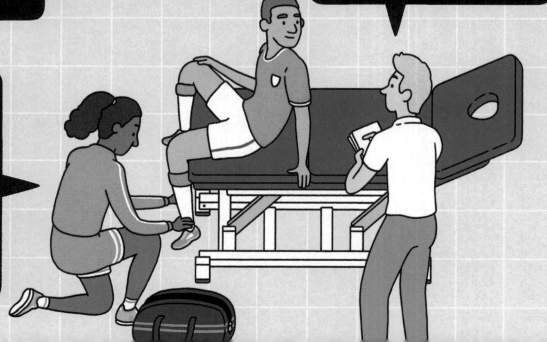

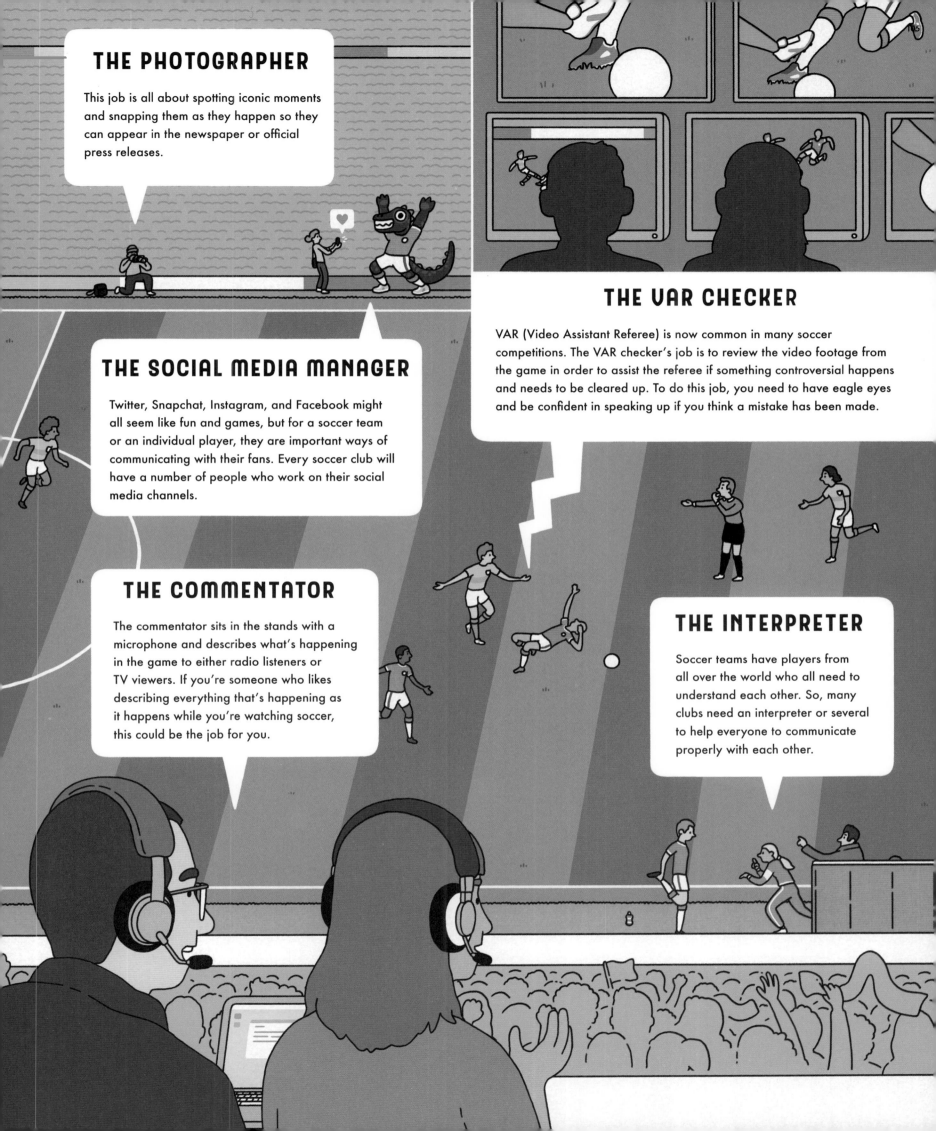

THE PHOTOGRAPHER

This job is all about spotting iconic moments and snapping them as they happen so they can appear in the newspaper or official press releases.

THE VAR CHECKER

VAR (Video Assistant Referee) is now common in many soccer competitions. The VAR checker's job is to review the video footage from the game in order to assist the referee if something controversial happens and needs to be cleared up. To do this job, you need to have eagle eyes and be confident in speaking up if you think a mistake has been made.

THE SOCIAL MEDIA MANAGER

Twitter, Snapchat, Instagram, and Facebook might all seem like fun and games, but for a soccer team or an individual player, they are important ways of communicating with their fans. Every soccer club will have a number of people who work on their social media channels.

THE COMMENTATOR

The commentator sits in the stands with a microphone and describes what's happening in the game to either radio listeners or TV viewers. If you're someone who likes describing everything that's happening as it happens while you're watching soccer, this could be the job for you.

THE INTERPRETER

Soccer teams have players from all over the world who all need to understand each other. So, many clubs need an interpreter or several to help everyone to communicate properly with each other.

THE GAME DAY

If you are going to watch a soccer game, whoever you're with, whoever you're watching play, and wherever you're watching it, it is an amazing experience. Around the world, everyone experiences soccer games in different ways. Many customs are similar; others are very specific to a particular place. There will always be a field and a ball and two teams, but sometimes there won't be a stand and sometimes there will be four stands that hold 100,000 people. Some people will have a pre-game hot dog, and others might have a burrito. All of these elements come together to make game day wonderful. There is a guide to what you might see, smell, and hear.

LEAVING HOME

Getting ready for the game is important: you need to dress appropriately…

You may want to wear your lucky scarf, or shirt, or pants. Although unfortunately, your team can still lose even if you are wearing all three lucky items.

Remember your tickets!

THE JOURNEY TO THE GAME

If you are driving to the game with your family or your friends, you can tune in to the pre-game build-up on the radio.

If you're catching the train, you might bump into lots of other soccer fans and talk about what you think is going to happen during the game and what you thought of the last game.

If you're taking the bus to the game, especially an away game, groups of fans will sing and cheer all the way to the game. This is lots of fun if you're a fan but probably a nightmare if you're a bus driver.

If you're walking to the game, listen as the noise of the crowd grows louder and louder as you approach!

PRE-GAME FOOD

There are all sorts of pre, during, and post-game foods around the globe. Here are some of the best:

Mexico Noodles with chilli and lime. People will come to your seat and sell you noodles at many soccer grounds in Mexico.

Russia & Spain Sunflower seeds and peanuts. These healthy little snacks are very popular, and as you leave the stadium, your feet crunch over the shells like fresh snow.

United Kingdom Pies. Hot pies (meat-filled pastries) are a classic soccer food in the UK, probably because they are very warming on a cold day spent outside!

Germany *Currywurst*. This is a boiled and fried sausage covered in curry sauce. They are utterly *wunderschön*.

Belgium *Frites* & mayonnaise. Belgium is famous for its *frites*, also known as fries.

USA Hot dogs. These are a game-day staple in the US, served with fried onions, mustard, and ketchup. Perfect.

PROGRAM AND SCARF SELLERS

On your way into the ground, you may see people selling programs or scarves. Programs often have lots of pictures and interviews with players, or a message from the team coach. They also have a list on the back of them with the names of all the players and their squad number, which makes it easier to figure out who scored that amazing goal if you're sitting miles away from the field. Scarves and programs are great souvenirs to have from a soccer game but they are not as important as your memories.

STEWARD

These guys make sure everything runs smoothly at the game and that everyone behaves. Important.

TICKET TAKER

You'll have to give this person your ticket. Although, more and more often stadiums have replaced the operators with machine turnstiles.

STADIUM ANNOUNCER

This person has a microphone connected to big speakers in the stadium. They'll announce the teams and goals and provide a bit of entertainment at halftime.

MASCOT

A person dressed in a big, often fluffy costume that represents your team. They are usually good at gymnastics, or running, or throwing prizes into the stands.

Soccer crowds are described in many ways by many people. Some people think they are like one huge family, and others say they are like churchgoers at their chapel, and others say they are a bunch of hooligans. One thing we can agree on is that without them, soccer would be nothing.

Songs and chants, generally, come and go with changing players and coaches. Many of them are witty or funny, but the best ones are simple and timeless. If you can think of a chant or song that applies to the team regardless of who the players or coaches are, then you've got a winner. There are some, however, that remain constant.

*"Walk on, walk on
With hope in your heart
And you'll never walk alone
You'll never walk alone."*

LIVERPOOL "YOU'LL NEVER WALK ALONE"

This is a song of togetherness winning over adversity. Liverpool fans sing it to a crescendo before every game they play. It has inspired many a famous win for the reds.

As well as the chants, the crowd expresses themselves with banners, posters, tifos, and wild dancing performances. Look out for these on terraces around the world.

ICELAND NATIONAL TEAM "THE VIKING CLAP"

Some chants have no words at all. At World Cup 2018 in Russia, the Icelandic fans often performed the thunderclap to spur on their team. The fans would clap once, all at the same time. One mega-loud clap. Then they'd do it again, leaving a shorter and shorter gap between each clap, speeding up, until the whole crowd was clapping, apparently like Vikings.

THE POZNAN / GRECQUE

A form of celebration where row upon row of fans turn their backs to the game, link arms and jump up and down at the same time. It looks like a huge wave, and it originated in Poland in 1961. Manchester City played a team called Poznan in 2010, saw their fans doing it, and decided to steal it.

THE YELLOW WALL

328 ft long and 131 ft high, Borussia Dortmund's stadium Westfalenstadion has a single stand full of 24,450 fans called Die Gelbe Wand—the Yellow Wall. The noise it makes is phenomenal, the colors are next level, and the huge banners that the fans make for each game, called tifos, are the best in the world.

DOING THE DAI

Llanelli Town is a semi-professional Welsh team, and Dai Chappell is their superfan. Born in 1944, Dai has gone to every Llanelli game for 25 years and is famous for his celebration. He often stands behind the goal on his own and throws both of his arms to the sky each time Llanelli score.

SOCCER SONGS IN POP CULTURE

Soccer songs have occasionally become popular beyond soccer and made it into the charts. This is especially common in World Cup years when nations adopt a song as their anthem for the tournament. "Three Lions" by Baddiel, Skinner, and the Lightning Seeds, "World In Motion" by New Order (featuring John Barnes's infamous rapping skills), and "Nessun Dorma," originally from the Puccini opera *Turandot*, are among the most popular of these.

INDEX

Abedi Pelé 46
Accrington 13
A.C. Milan 13, 26, 52, 56, 71, 73
AFC Asian Cup 47
African Cup of Nations 46
Agüero, Sergio 21
Ajax 16, 28–9, 37, 41, 81
Akers, Michelle 13, 28, 45, 48, 91
Alba, Jordi 37
Alberto, Carlos 23, 61
A-League 48
Algarve Cup 19
Algeria 46
Alonso, Xabi 74–5
Ancelotti, Carlo 39, 52
Anfield 39
Argentina 12, 22, 31, 44, 53, 73, 97–8
Arsenal 14, 20, 48, 71, 81, 91, 95
AS Adema 96
Aston Villa 13
Atlético Madrid 73
Australia 48, 63, 96
Ayew, Abedi see Abedi Pelé
Ayew, André 46
Ayew, Ibrahim 46
Ayew, Jordan 46

Baggio, Roberto 57
Ball, Alan 21
Ballon d'Or 18, 26, 29–30
Balotelli, Mario 95
Bangladesh 6
Barcelona 6–7, 20, 28–9, 31, 37–8, 42, 46, 48, 52, 82–3, 96
Baresi, Franco 52
Barnes, John 109
Barrios, Daniel Alberto Villalva 97
Bayern Munich 27, 52, 75
Bebeto 92
Beckenbauer, Franz 27, 61
Beckham, David 7, 40, 48, 72–3, 90
Belgium 6, 14, 87, 107
Benitez, Rafa 19
Bent, Darren 97
Bergkamp, Dennis 53, 80–1
Berisha, Besart 48
Birmingham 95
Bishop Auckland 39
Blackburn Rovers 13
Blackpool 30
Boca Juniors 53, 61
Bolton Wanderers 13
Bolt, Usain 48
Bombonera, la 53
Bordeaux 29
Borussia Dortmund 55, 109
Botswana 6
Brazil 6, 12–3, 23, 30–1, 44–5,

57, 91–2, 96–7, 99
Bronze, Lucy 18
Bull, Steve 92
Bundesliga 75
Burnley 13
Busquets, Sergio 17, 37
Butt, Nicky 40

Calabash, the see Soccer City
Camara, Moussa 97
Cameroon 46, 90, 94, 99
Campbell, Sol 71
Camp Nou 52, 96
Cannes 29
Cantona, Eric 31, 94
Carlos, Roberto 29
Casillas, Iker 56
Central Coast Mariners 48
Champions League 13, 15, 17–20, 26–7, 29, 37–9, 48, 52, 54, 56, 63, 71, 75, 83
Chan Yuen Ting 41
Chelsea 30, 69, 83, 85, 95
China 12–3, 27–8, 48, 98
Chinese Super League 48
Clermont Foot 41
Clough, Brian 27
Collina, Pierluigi 103
Colombia 90
Colombo, Angelo 52
CONCACAF Cup 19
Congo 46
Congo-Kinshasa 46
Copa América 47
Copa del Rey 17, 36, 48, 75
Copa Libertadores 31
Costacurta, Alessandro 52
Croatia 71
Crouch, Peter 95
Cruyff, Johan 10, 16, 21, 28–9, 36–8, 60
Cuba 65
Cup Winners Cup 39
Czech Republic 99

da Silva, Marta Vieira 30, 45
Death, Steve 97
de Boer, Frank 53
de Lima, Ronaldo see Ronaldo
Del Piero, Alessandro 26, 55
Denmark 62
de Oliveira, José Roberto Gama see Bebeto
Derby County 13
DFB-Pokal 75
Diacre, Corinne 41
Dick, Kerr Ladies 12, 14
Di Stéfano, Alfredo 15
Division 1 Féminine 48
Donadoni, Roberto 52

do Nascimento, Edson Arantes see Pelé
Drogba, Didier 84–5
Dulwich Hamlet 97
Dynamo Kyiv 39
Dynamo Moscow 26

Eastern Sports Club 41
East Stirlingshire 40
Egypt 12, 46
England 7, 13, 15, 18, 21, 30, 44, 48, 54, 63, 71, 73, 91, 95
Eredivisie 29, 36
Estonia 64
Ethiopia 46
European Championships 16, 27, 36, 46, 75
European Cup 12, 15–6, 27, 36, 39, 46, 52
European Super Cup 39
Eusebio 26
Everton 13

Fàbregas, Cesc 37
FA Cup 14, 30, 38, 40, 52, 54
Fawcett, Joy 27
FAWSL 48
Ferguson, Sir Alex 9, 39–40
Ferreira, Eusebio da Silva see Eusebio
Feyenoord 28
Finland 98
First National Bank Stadium see Soccer City
Football League 13
Formiga 45
France 18, 23, 29, 44–5, 48, 53, 60, 63, 65, 87, 91

Galácticos 15, 19
Galli, Filippo 52
Garrincha, Mané 12
Genk 87
Gento, Francisco 15
Germany 16, 23, 27, 44–6, 54–5, 95, 107
Ghana 46, 79
Giggs, Ryan 40
Giroud, Olivier 91
Giuseppe Meazza Stadium see San Siro
Golden Boot 28
Gold Pride 30
Greaves, Jimmy 48
Grêmio 62
Grosso, Fabio 55
Guangzhou Evergrande Taobao 48
Guardiola, Pep 29, 36, 38

Gullitt, Ruud 52

Hamburger SV 27
Hamm, Mia 19, 28
Hegerberg, Ada 18, 48
Henry, Amandine 18
Henry, Thierry 22
Hernández, Xavi see Xavi
Herrera, Ander 10
Hong Kong Premier League 41
Hughes, Mark 40
Hungary 15, 95
Hurst, Geoff 54

Ibrahimović, Zlatan 29
Iceland 108
INAC Kobe Leonessa 69
Ince, Paul 40
Iniesta, Andrés 17, 37, 82
Inter Miami 48
Inter Milan 56
Iraq 47
Italy 12–3, 23, 26, 44, 48, 55, 57, 61, 63, 71, 73, 87, 99
Ivory Coast 46, 85

Japan 45, 47–8, 64–5, 98
Ji So-yun 68–9
J-League 48
Jørgensen, Simon Bloch 97
Juventus 20, 29, 48, 61

Kaizer Chiefs FC 56
Kanchelskis, Andrei 40
Kane, Harry 45
Kansas City 48
Kashima Antlers 48
Kerr, Samantha 48
Klinsmann, Jürgen 95
KNVB Cup 36
Kopa, Raymond 15
Koulibaly, Kalidou 86–7
Kovács, Stefán 16

LA Galaxy 48, 73
La Liga 12, 17, 29, 36–7, 48, 75
La Masia 37
Lazio 61
League Cup 38, 40
Ledesma, Pedro Eliezer Rodríguez see Pedro
Leeds 95
Le Mans 85
Le Sommer, Eugénie 18
Le Tissier, Matt 76–7
Levante 28
Leverkusen 29
Ligue 1 18, 48
Lilleshall 71
Lilly, Kristine 19

Lippi, Marcello 48
Liverpool 13, 39, 74–5, 97, 108
Ljungkvist, Adam Lindin 97
Llanelli Town 109
Lobanovskyi, Valeriy 39
Los Angeles Aztecs 28
Lyon see Olympique Lyonnais

Madureira Sporting Club 65
Makélélé, Claude 35
Maldini, Cesare 26
Maldini, Paolo 26, 52
Manchester City 36, 38, 54, 62, 95, 109
Manchester United 9, 31, 40, 48, 52, 73, 95
Maracanã, Estadio do 44, 96
Maradona, Diego 21, 35, 44, 48
Marseille see Olympique de Marseille
Mascherano, Javier 31
Matthews, Sir Stanley 30
Meijer, Henny 48
Melbourne Cricket Ground 54, 96
Melbourne Victory 48
Messi, Lionel 10, 12, 17, 31, 37–8, 48, 77
Metz 87
Mexico 44, 64, 107
Michels, Rinus 16, 36–7
Miedema, Vivianne 48
Milburn, Jackie 21
Milla, Roger 13, 94
Milner, James 35
MLS 48
Modeste, Anthony 95
Monaco 20
Montoya, Martín 37
Moore, Bobby 54
Morocco 46
Mota, Miraildes Maciel see Formiga
Mukura Victory 97
Múnera, Gerardo Alberto Bedoya 97

Nagoya Grampus Eight 64
Napoli 87
Nchout, Ajara 90
Neeskens, Johan 28
Nesta, Alessandro 70–1
Netherlands 28, 53, 60, 62
Neville, Gary 40, 83
Neville, Phil 40
Newcastle United 21, 75
Newell's Old Boys 31
New York Cosmos 27, 31, 61
New York Red Bulls 20
Nigeria 46, 65, 90

Norway 13, 45, 90, 99
Nottingham Forest 27
Notts County 13, 95
NWSL 48

Ōkubo, Yoshito 48
Old Trafford 94
Olympic Games 12–3, 15–6, 19, 47, 52, 54, 90
Olympique de Marseille 46, 53, 60, 63, 65, 85
Olympique Lyonnais 48
Olympique Lyonnais Féminin 10, 12, 18, 41, 48
Onnis, Delio 48
Orlando Lions Women 28
Orlando Pride 30
Özil, Mesut 6

Paisley, Bob 39
Parris, Nikita 48
Pavard, Benjamin 23
Pedro 39
Pelé 12, 22–3, 31, 97
Perth Glory 48
Piola, Silvio 48
Piqué, Gerard 37
Pirlo, Andrea 20
Platini, Michel 61
Plymouth Argyle 60
Pogba, Paul 90
Poland 109
Portland Thorns 48
Poznan 109
Prandelli, Cesare 61
Premier League 13–4, 20, 38, 48, 52, 73, 97
Preston North End 13–4
Prinz, Birgit 16
Puskás, Ferenc 10, 15
Puyol, Carles 37

Rapinoe, Megan 94
Rayon Sport 97
Reading 97
Real Madrid 12, 15, 19, 29, 48, 54, 73, 75
Real Sociedad 75
Reina, Pepe 97
Renard, Wendie 18
Rijkaard, Frank 52
Rimet, Jules 44, 54
Robson, Sir Bobby 10, 38
Romania 91
Ronaldinho 20, 91
Ronaldo 20, 91
Ronaldo, Cristiano 77
Rool, Cyril 97
Rose Bowl, the 57, 96
Rozeira, Cristiane 55

Rungrado 1st of May Stadium 96
Russia 23, 26, 60, 90, 107–8

Sacchi, Arrigo 52
Saint-Étienne 48
Sampdoria 63
San Diego Spirit 27
San Siro 56
Santos 31
Sarri, Maurizio 87
Saudi Arabia 47
Scholes, Paul 40
Seaman, David 91
Sebes, Gusztáv 15
Serie A 12, 26, 29, 48, 71
Shankly, Bill 39
Shearer, Alan 21, 48, 92
She Believes Cup 19
Sheffield Wednesday 95
Sheringham, Teddy 52
Signal Iduna Park see Westfalenstadion
Simeone, Diego 73
Soccer City 56, 96
Socceroos 96
SO L'Emyrne 96
Solskjaer, Ole Gunnar 52
South Africa 12, 30, 46, 56, 96
South African Premier Soccer League 56
Southampton 77
South Korea 69
Soviet Union 26, 39, 60
Spain 12, 15, 17, 19, 44, 46, 48, 61, 73, 82, 96, 107
Stadium of Light, the 97
St Helen's Ladies 12, 14
Stoke City 13, 30
Suárez, Luis 78–9
Sudan 46
Sunderland 97
Sweden 90, 97

Tardelli, Marco 61
Tasmania 54
Tassotti, Mauro 52
tiki-taka 17, 46
Tokyo Verdy 48
Torres, Fernando 83
Total Football 10, 16, 28–9, 36–7, 41
Tottenham Hotspur 54–5, 95
Totti, Francesco 20
Trinidad and Tobago 99
Tunisia 46
Tyresö FF 28

UCF Knights 48
UEFA Cup 39
Ukraine 39

Umeå IK 30
United Arab Republic 46
Uruguay 12, 22, 44, 47, 79, 96
USA 13–4, 19–20, 27–8, 45, 48, 61, 64, 73, 92, 94, 96, 107
USSR see Soviet Union

Valderrama, Carlos 90
Valdés, Víctor 37
van Basten, Marco 52
van Nistelrooy, Ruud 9
Vasco da Gama 30
Vélodrome, the 53
Victoria 54

Waddle, Chris 90
Wambach, Abby 19
Washington Diplomats 28
Wembley Stadium 15, 54, 69
Wenger, Arsène 14, 64
West Bromwich Albion 13
Westfalenstadion 55, 109
West Germany 15, 27, 54, 62
West, Taribo 90
White, Ellen 95
White Hart Lane 54–5
Wolverhampton Wanderers 13, 92
Women's FA 12
Women's FA Cup 13
Women's World Cup 12–3, 16, 19, 27–8, 30, 45, 65, 94–5
Wondolowski, Chris 48
World Cup 6, 12–3, 15, 17, 20–3, 26–7, 29, 31, 44, 46, 48, 52–7, 63, 65, 71, 73, 75, 79, 91–2, 94–6, 108–9
Wu Lei 48
WUSA 27

Xavi 17, 37, 82

Yashin, Lev 26

Zaire 46
Zambia 46
Zidane, Zinedine 19–20, 29, 39
Zola, Gianfranco 30

Brimming with creative inspiration, how-to projects, and useful information to enrich your everyday life, Quarto Knows is a favorite destination for those pursuing their interests and passions. Visit our site and dig deeper with our books into your area of interest: Quarto Creates, Quarto Cooks, Quarto Homes, Quarto Lives, Quarto Drives, Quarto Explores, Quarto Gifts, or Quarto Kids.

Inspiring | Educating | Creating | Entertaining

The Big Book of Football by Mundial © 2020 Quarto Publishing plc
Text © 2020 Mundial
Illustrations © 2020 Damien Weighill

First Published in 2020 by Wide Eyed Editions, an imprint of The Quarto Group.
400 First Avenue North, Suite 400, Minneapolis, MN 55401, USA.
T (612) 344-8100 F (612) 344-8692 www.QuartoKnows.com

The right of Mundial to be identified as the author and Damien Weighill to be identified as the illustrator of this work has been asserted by them in accordance with the Copyright, Designs and Patents Act, 1988 (United Kingdom).

A catalog record for this book is available from the British Library.

ISBN 978-0-7112-4910-3

The illustrations were created digitally
Set in Mexcellent 3D, Futura and Hipton Sans

Published by Georgia Amson-Bradshaw
Designed by Myrto Dimitrakoulia
Edited by Lucy Brownridge

Manufactured in Guangdong, China CC112019

9 8 7 6 5 4 3 2 1

MIX
Paper from responsible sources
FSC® C008047
www.fsc.org